D1055077

# Blow-Drying the Frog & Other Parenting Adventures

edited by Laura M. Jones,
from the pages of *Welcome Home*®

Published by Family and Home Network™
Fairfax, Virginia

Cover illustrations by Odin K. Smith

Interior illustrations by Cathleen F. Gardner

© 2002 by Family and Home Network

Typesetting by FreeStyle Publications

Blow-drying the frog & other parenting adventures / edited by Laura M.
Jones, from the pages of Welcome home.
    p. cm.
 ISBN 0-9631188-3-8
 1. Parenting. 2. Parent and child. 3. Parenting--Humor. 4. Parent
and child--Humor. I. Title: Blow-drying the frog and other parenting
adventures. II. Jones, Laura M. (Laura McNeill), 1955- III. Welcome
home.
HQ755.8.B62 2002
649'.1--dc21

                 2002151419

# Contents

# We're in This Together ...................... 53

# Someday We'll Laugh ...................... 89

# No One Warned Me! ...............................119

# Coming to Terms ............................. 209

# About Family and Home Network ............................. 223

# Foreword
## by Laura M. Jones

Parenting is a serious business. At each stage of our parenting journey, there are important decisions to be made and important problems to handle. Our children are growing up in a scary world, and they have to be prepared.

But in the midst of this parenting work, it helps to be reminded of how much fun it is to be a parent—how much our children can make us laugh, how often they get us into funny situations, and just how joyful time with our children can be. Sometimes we can get the joke right away, but other times seeing the humor takes some perspective. Sometimes lots of perspective. In fact, the only saving grace to some situations is the knowledge that it will make a good story to laugh about later—like maybe next year.

Children learn by trying things out and making mistakes, and clearly parents make mistakes too. We get distracted and leave a small child with an amazing rock standing next to a forest green van (see "Smiley Faces"). We decide to make delicious applesauce without considering our sewer system ("The Great Applesauce Adventure") and we leave a water glass full of sea-monkeys sitting on our kitchen counter ("Sea Monkeys and Billable Hours"). Despite our best efforts to organize our children and homes, things get out of control ("The Laundry Dance"). And sometimes unpredictable things happen, and we're just along for the ride ("The Move").

In the midst of our struggles to raise strong, happy families, we need to appreciate the funny moments. Scientists say that laughing reduces stress, releases positive hormones and is good for our internal organs—it's just healthy. Most of us have had the experience of having a friend phone in the middle of a bad day—as we recount all the mundane irritations and share our frustrations, suddenly our moods lift. We can laugh together over that incident at the grocery store. Her children have done the same annoying thing.

That is what this book is intended to be—a group of friends sharing the humorous aspects of their day with you. It's that voice on the other end of the phone line reminding you that you're not alone in facing the joys and worries of raising children, that it's okay to lighten up. That yes, being a parent is a tough job—but it can also be pretty darn funny.

# Acknowledgments

As with every effort of our nonprofit organization, Family and Home Network, this project was completed through the collaborative work of many people. Most of us read stories, proofread pages or helped with correspondence with the nagging feeling that we really should be fixing dinner, checking homework or doing the laundry. Somehow, together, we managed to keep our families and our organization running while producing our monthly journal, *Welcome Home*, and this book.

First and foremost, appreciation goes to Cathy Myers, the executive director of Family and Home Network, for her deep devotion and years of hard work in support of children and families. Her expertise and commitment, along with a good sense of humor, have been our guiding star.

Next my sincere appreciation goes to Cathy Gardner, our art director, for her calm acceptance of our vacillating ideas and vague suggestions. She did a wonderful job, and miraculously never threw anything at us.

Special thanks go to Terri Scullen, who searched our archives for good material and helped with correspondence, and to Eileen Doughty, who also searched for good stories, provided invaluable help in getting material reviewed and kept me going when distractions threatened to derail me. (Thanks also, Eileen, for sharing your screened-in porch and those margaritas.)

Appreciation goes to the Board of Directors of Family and Home Network for their enthusiastic backing of this project. They understand how important it is to laugh.

The poems come to us courtesy of our poetry editor, Winnie Cross, whose dedication over many years has kept the pages of *Welcome Home* graced with lyrical, heartwarming, and sometimes funny poems.

Thanks are also due to Marian Gormley, Susan De Ritis, Nancy Boselovic, Nancy Vazquez, Jackie Codevilla, Nancy Robinson, Clare Anderson, Maureen Flanagan-Johnson, Mandy Book, Julia Marcois, Laurie Tasharski, Eileen Mallon, Connie Winkler, Anna Mary Warden, Jennie Reinhart and Allison Woodward for their support, encouragement and help in reviewing our material. It's probably good that they all have different senses of humor. Eileen Doughty, Donna DeSoto and Marybeth Connelly contributed wonderful proof-reading skills, and Barbara Cornwell's help with correspondence was much appreciated.

And as always, our deep thanks go to the authors, poets and illustrators of *Welcome Home*. Their heartfelt, moving, poignant and hilarious writings and artwork have enriched us all.

—*Laura M. Jones*

# Everyday
# Chaos

# Why I Still Practice Lamaze

### by Rosemary Raymond Horvath

I just finished scrubbing the kitchen floor. It was an emergency: I was afraid that if I didn't clean the floor, somebody would get stuck and we'd have to call 911 to save him. It is a terrible thing to let things get out of hand like that, but that is my life. Of course, the trouble with a clean floor is that somebody is going to want to walk on it. I got so upset about someone stepping on my clean floor that I actually yelled at a child for playing in the kitchen play area. Those blocks were messing up my floor!

Unfortunately, the endless patience that mothers display doesn't show. A clean floor does. On a day when we crave approval—or cleanliness—we will wantonly throw out patience to get it. Say you have company coming, a time-honored occasion that requires a certain amount of cleanliness. You want to have a clean house, a fresh pot of coffee, a plate of goodies and well-scrubbed children. What will surely happen, instead, is that one of your children will spill Karo® syrup on the kitchen floor and try to clean it up with cold water while you answer the door. Most of the Karo syrup will stay on the floor, but some will transfer to your child, the walls, the curtains, the company and so on.

I recall the time that some ladies from my church were coming over. I had lectured my children to the point that they were lined up on the couch quietly reading books while I finished up in the kitchen. One of my sons went to the bathroom, and in an effort to "freshen the air" he dumped an entire bottle of Oscar de la Renta perfume down the toilet. Well, his motives were pure!

The point is, simply being a mother requires patience you never knew you had. The fact that it takes nearly a year to gestate is the first clue. If you adopt children, it isn't exactly something you do over the weekend on a whim either. Getting children requires patience. Raising them requires heroic patience. The best patience is when you don't know you are being patient, but there are ways to develop patience. I think I have stumbled upon one of these ways: Lamaze classes. I have long felt that the Lamaze classes taught to expectant mothers are not designed to remove the pain of childbirth; that's hogwash. I have had six babies, and I can tell you, it's a big ouch. But Lamaze training has stopped me from going nuts because of those six babies. I do that deep breathing, relax, and then mop up with a smile. Lamaze is one of the best things that ever happened to me. It helps in slow checkout lines, too.

Don't misunderstand. I enjoy my children enormously. They are the light of my world. My husband and I wonder what we would ever talk about if we didn't have such interesting progeny. But we all know that listening to a toddler articulate big ideas is deeply

rewarding—if we have the patience to listen. Listening to a teenager is similarly fascinating. It will take her two hours to describe an hour-and-a-half movie, but during that time you might just hear how her ideas are forming, too. I pray each day for patience. Without patience, this job wouldn't be any fun!

But my house would be cleaner.

# Mom, I Can Dress Myself!

First underwear
(inside out, but who will see?)
Then shirt
(no problem there, the sweater will cover the label
only showing slightly beneath your chin)
Your skirt goes on with greatest ease.
Tights are next
(the heels on top, oops, you can fix that)
Now twisted,
(but who looks that closely?)
You sigh with satisfaction,
Glowing with pride
All dressed for the day, without any help!
You are ready now to leave,
(but I must wipe my eyes before we go).

*Lynn Vogt Adams*

# Mindbenders for Moms

## by Gayle Urban

**R**ead each of the following problems carefully, then determine your solutions. You may go back at any time to double-check your answers, but remember that you will be judged on both accuracy and speed. Begin. (A No. 2 pencil is recommended; however, crayon stubs are acceptable.)

1. The post office is four miles away; its hours are 8:30 a.m. to 4:40 p.m. You have two baby gifts, one birthday present (already belated) and the car registration to mail. Passengers accompanying you on this errand will include a) a small infant, b) a toddler and c) an older child. The infant naps at 10 a.m., 2 p.m. and 4 p.m.; the toddler naps at 12:30 p.m. The older child does not nap but droops considerably from 1:30 to 2:30 in the afternoon. The infant nurses at 8:30 and 11:30 in the morning and at 1:00, 1:30, 3:30, 3:45 and 4:15 in the afternoon. The toddler and the older child eat at 12 noon and will die without a snack at 3 p.m. Vehicle loading time is seven-and-a-half seconds per pound. **Question:** What time will you go to the post office? (Allow twelve minutes for traffic.)

Bonus points: Prepare conclusive evidence to explain to your spouse why the packages and the mail still are sitting on the shelf in the hallway.

2. It is 97 degrees outside with a humidity factor of 88 percent. Grass is withering at the rate of one square

7

inch every five minutes. Talk the four-year-old out of wearing his Superman sweatshirt.

3. There are graham crackers and a box of Cracker Jacks® for snacks. Convince the two-year-old that he gets a cracker.

4. "Early to bed and early to rise makes a man healthy, wealthy and wise." Translate this into words that a child will accept.

5. Cartoons come on the TV at 3:30 p.m. Five minutes later the station interrupts its regularly scheduled program for a special news update. Discuss, at a preschooler's level, the pros (and cons) of cartoons vs. the President of the United States. (You may use visual aids.)

6. Son A wants a pair of sixty-nine dollar sneakers. Son B needs sixty-nine dollars worth of orthodontic work. Explain to Son A the concept "things might be the same but things aren't always equal." Give yourself bonus points if you can smile through straight teeth as you explain this.

7. There are seven boxes of breakfast cereal on the shelf. Your child believes that "there isn't any good cereal" in the house. Convince him otherwise.

8. When scoring the above, give yourself bonus points if you were able to finish without being interrupted five times. Build up your final score by adding an extra point for every hand you hold, spirit you lift and problem you solve today.

Looking at other people's answers is permitted and guessing is inevitable. Good luck!

# Buying Time

### by Lorie Shane

**W**ith my two-year-old son bedded down for his afternoon nap, I make a mental list of what I still need to do today. Two loads of laundry to wash and three to fold. Ironing (maybe). Exercise. Finish making valentines. Sew a tuck in son's pants. Dinner. Playtime with son. Conversation time with husband. Call Mom. Look through mail.

It never ends, I think as I try to set priorities. It's like this every day. There is just never enough time. And please—I've had enough advice on how to be more efficient. My recipe box is crammed with thirty-minute recipe ideas. I use every cleaning shortcut I know. I trade off babysitting with other mothers. Let's face it. What the mothers of this country really need is a way to buy time. We already borrow it, beg it and steal it. What if we could pick it up at the corner market?

I have an idea how it might work. All I know is that it would be 5:00 in the afternoon, and I would open up a package of time and set it on my dining room table. Then my son and I would finish playing with dough, I would wash our hands, clear the dining room table of the assorted things that had gathered there that day and put together a casserole, stopping several times to change my son's pants, find a toy that "isn't anywhere" and pretend to be Mr. McFeely to his Mr. Rogers. As I did this I would take the time to put recyclable things in

9

recycling boxes, spread wet towels out to dry instead of leaving them in lumps, and pick up crumbs as I walk by them instead of pretending not to notice. Then I would look at the clock and it would be—5:15.

Just think. As you look over the calendar for the coming week, you would note that you have a hair appointment on Wednesday, play group on Thursday (your turn to host) and your husband's soccer game Thursday night. You owe letters to several people, it's time to plant the flower garden and you promised to make seafood fettucine for dinner one night. Oh dear, you might say, I'd better buy extra time this week. In my fantasy, it would be available at the deli counter: "I'd like a quarter pound of turkey breast, half a pound of Muenster, and oh, about ninety minutes."

Of course, it would also come prepackaged at convenience stores, so on "those" days you could call your husband at work and say, "Honey, could you pick up some time on the way home?" This is not to mention that all of the money machines located next to banks would be remodeled to dispense time, too, and every mother would be issued a plastic time card so she could buy time after hours.

I would try to buy second-hand time when I could. Let's say somebody had used about twenty minutes for peeling potatoes. I could buy that time and use it over again for making phone calls, keeping an eye on my son in the sandbox and scouring the kitchen sink, be-

cause everybody knows that mothers can do all of those things at the same time.

Not that I would be a time hog. The reasonable part of me knows that we only get twenty-four hours a day because it forces us to decide what's really important in life right now. I don't think it would be right to buy enough time to go on safari, finish my master's degree or write my first novel. But is it too much to be able to read *all* the newspaper and finish my exercise video, including the cool down?

I could go on and on, but even as I write, I know there are dishes to wash, bills to pay and a son who needs his mother for story time. Then again, if you could just hold on a minute, I could go open that package of time...

# A Crayon Spill

Box of crayons— sixty four
dumped onto the kitchen floor;
cherry pink and tangerine,
silver, tan and forest green.

Lemon yellow, skin-like peach,
lavender rolled out of reach;
orchid, turquoise, blue and plum,
transformed white linoleum.

An oil, gas or water spill
creates a mess which makes man ill,
but I approved this rollaway—
a crayon spill colorized my day.

*Connie Bretz*

# Pennies in the Soap Dish

### by Renee Hawkley

**N**ot every household has twenty-seven pennies in the soap dish. Ours hasn't always had them, either, but it does today. Come to think of it, if you haven't visited us in a while, you might have a few questions. Let me tell you right away, I can explain everything.

I suppose an average visitor might wonder about the pennies. My daughter, Janette (age seven), had to wash them, she said, because they were dirty. They were dirty because a couple of summers ago, somebody in the house with twenty-seven pennies to spare threw them out the bedroom window, and they landed in a flower bed. Unfortunately, they failed to germinate and sprout into penny trees, and yesterday Ethan (age ten) discovered the buried treasure in the flower bed and gave them to Janette, and that's why we have pennies in the soap dish.

You might take a look at our cat, Tigger, and wonder what he's doing with a bandage tied around his head. Well, Tigger and Spice, the cat next door, are not best friends. The only thing they agree on is that birds don't belong on our property. Unfortunately, Tigger is smaller and a little less cunning, and so when Tigger and Spice tangle, Tigger always loses. Last time he came home with a bloody head; hence, the bandage.

Next, you may wonder why all the wastebaskets are on the counters and chests of drawers instead of on the floor, where normal wastebaskets would be. Well, it's because I'm babysitting a pair of eight-month-old twins lately, and all the goodies in the wastebaskets are just what eight-month-old twins love to play with the best.

What are the ice cream containers of rocks doing on the porch? Actually, they've been there for the better part of a year, awaiting the day when they can have rose petals, feathers and a sprinkle of sand added for rose petal stew.

So you noticed the rug on the piano bench. It's there because nobody, but nobody (including me) likes to practice the piano on an old, hard bench, and the rug is one of those soft, homemade "Grandma things" that makes sitting and playing the piano a pleasure.

Yes, there are rubber bands scattered all over the driveway. When the boys go out on their early morning paper routes, they drop rubber bands and "forget" to pick them up when they get home.

Why is there a pile of games in the hall? Frankly, because there just isn't room for them until someone who has a little more time than I do rearranges the mess in the closet so they can fit.

And there's a laundry basket full of clean, white socks in the laundry room. The job everybody in the house hates the most is matching socks, so we save it for people who mess up, and lately everybody has been relatively well-behaved. It's a sorry situation when a

mother has to hope that someone will act up fairly soon so she won't have to match the socks.

I suppose that brings me to the question I know you've been dying to ask. You want to know why a forty-six-year-old woman of reasonable intelligence and maturity is wearing a white barrette with little duckies on the side to hold her hair out of her eyes. That's easy. It's because the pink barrette with the little elephants doesn't match my outfit.

## Re-entry

Overdue books are calling
and I simply must get to the store,
while suitcases yet to be emptied
grace the middle of the kitchen floor;
and I hear the doorbell ringing,
as I muse with resignation,
"How come I feel so tired…
All I did was go on vacation!"

*Gayle Urban*

# Rush Hour

## by Rosemary Raymond Horvath

**I**f I ever buy another house, it will have only one door. I say this after getting four of my six children off to school.

I sit in my command module (the swivel rocker in the living room) and nurse the baby while my children prepare for school. As one runs up the stairs in search of homework, another is wheeling bicycles out of the garage for himself and his brother. My teenage daughter needs to have her hair French-braided, and nobody is even impressed that I can do this while I nurse a baby.

I remind the children of their chores. Did they make their beds? Will I be able to tell if they did? Did they tidy up the bathroom? I don't care *whose* towel it is; hang it up! Did they tidy their bedrooms? Will I be able to tell if they did? Did they comb their hair? I can't tell!

The minutes tick by. My three-year-old suddenly requires teeth-flossing lessons from our resident expert, the six-year-old. This is a child so into tying knots that flossing counts as recreation. Naturally the flossing lesson happens in the living room. More children gather around, brushing their teeth, to watch. My twelve-year-old puts his toothbrush on the coffee table to help teach. (I will find the toothbrush later on, when guests arrive for coffee.)

I become more tense. Will my teenager catch the bus? Will the boys make it to school? Will we lose the

three-year-old again? They pick up the tempo as my voice rises. One child is looking in the back yard for his math book. Another is in the garage looking for a jacket. Another is upstairs, reading, oblivious to the clock. Another is looking for the one who is looking for the math book. Another is hoping for a different breakfast than what is on the table. I am looking for sanity.

Finally, they leave. All three outside doors slam simultaneously. I heave a sigh of relief. I go into the kitchen to clear up the breakfast dishes, then upstairs to get dirty clothes. But there is the bookworm! He forgot to go to school!

If I ever buy another house, it will have only one door. That way, I'll know who left!

# In the Car in Twenty Minutes

### by Joyce McPherson

If you have more than one child, people may have already asked you, "How *do* you do it?" Most of us modestly shrug or laugh and say, "I really don't know."

Recently I decided, for the sake of modern Mommy science, to record how I do one of my most frequent tasks: loading four children and a newborn baby into the car. The results were illuminating. The secret is to begin early, preferably twenty-four hours early. However, since that is usually impractical, twenty minutes works well enough. I call all my children together, look them squarely in the eye, and say firmly, "It's time to go."

This causes a flurry of activity. I explain to some of them, still in their pajamas, that they need to get dressed. (This is not always apparent to them.)

Next I begin piling the diaper bag, my purse, books for the car and anything else necessary for this particular trip (like a grocery list, a picnic lunch or library books) in front of the door from which I will leave. On good days I remember to check that my diaper bag is packed with necessities like diapers. Sometimes, I even find a change of clothes, diaper wipes, pacifiers and a bottle to put in the bag. By this time, more of the children are dressed. I remind them that they also need to put on their shoes and socks. I exhort those who are

still in pajamas to get ready. It is very tempting to say, "Get ready *now* or you will be left behind!" But I know I can't really do that. Instead, I try to remain calm and use simple instructions like "Put on this dress and stand next to the door."

Then I perform a few mental calisthenics to calculate if the baby's feeding time will intersect my driving time. Feeding the baby sets our departure back by a few minutes, but it allows me to sit on the couch and give the children directions: "Don't forget to brush your hair. There are clean socks in the dryer."

When I am done feeding the baby, I place him in his car seat, still in the house, but I don't buckle him in yet. At last, the moment of truth arrives. There is no turning back. I take a moment to evaluate which of the children is most likely to bolt out the door and play in the mud. I help that child put on his shoes, and I accompany him to the car. Though we will not leave for a few more minutes, I buckle his seat belt. (I learned this lesson the hard way. It's a long story, but we managed to reattach the rear view mirror in the end.) Then I repeat this step with the next child. By the time two children are in the car, at least one of the remaining children will remember that she has to use the bathroom.

I use this slight delay to check that everyone is indeed dressed, including myself. I check that my shoes match, my skirt zipper is in the back, I'm wearing a slip, my hair and teeth are brushed, and all facings are neatly tucked in. Then I quickly transfer the mountain of bags and things into the car. (A box works well for

transporting everything at once.) I call to all remaining children to get in the car, and tell the oldest one to check that everyone is buckled in. The cherry on the top of all my endeavors is the baby. Whoops! Yes, that is why I didn't buckle him in earlier. I change him, buckle him into his car seat, tuck a blanket around him and finally take him out to the car. If by some miracle I am ahead of schedule, I use the spare minutes to whisk through the house and turn off lights and any faucets that are still on. Finally, I get into the car, take a cleansing breath and turn the key in the ignition. We're ready! Now if only I could remember where we're going!

# Perspectives

# New Attitude

## by Barb Warner

**I** had a bad attitude. At the end of the day, my husband would walk through the door and ask, "What did you do today?" and I wanted to scream, "What did I do today? I cleaned—can't you tell?!"

Honestly, no one ever could tell. When I had an occasional burst of cleaning energy, the house would be clean for half an hour. Then the kids would come home from school or take things out or friends would come over to play, and we'd be right back where we started.

My bad attitude came partly from feeling that if I was a mother at home, my house should be tidy. If it wasn't clean and orderly, I felt it reflected poorly on me. That made me cranky.

For years I coped by cleaning, not cleaning, feeling inadequate, whining, not opening the door when people knocked and keeping the shades down. I read the home organization books and tried those cleaning techniques and, you know, *they worked*—for about a week. If I had kept following them, they'd be working today. But I didn't follow them. I quit. I was a quitter, a housework quitter.

It's taken me years to say that, but now I can and it's okay. What has brought me to this point is a resolution I made a few years ago. Actually it was more of a prayer than a resolution. I asked that either I be motivated to keep the house clean or I learn to live with it (and me) as is. In other words, do it or quit complaining.

I'd love to say I suddenly had the energy and initiative to keep my house clean. I didn't. I wish I could say I had a revelation and suddenly didn't care about my housekeeping reputation in the community. I care. But now, several years later, I realize my attitude has changed toward my home and my chores.

I stopped buying the books and attending the seminars, and I now refuse to live by organized people's high ideals. I have set my own standards, and in the process have found there are many housekeeping myths that need to be challenged. Let me share a few.

A friend once told me you should vacuum one day a week for each member of your family. No way! Vacuuming is only really necessary when dog hair is sticking to the baby's blanket sleeper. Since I don't have babies in the house anymore, this really saves me time. If our dog would run away, I'd be home free. The exception to this rule is when company is coming over and all the contiguous, carpeted rooms that can be vacuumed without switching outlets are free of toys and other debris. That happened once last year.

When you do vacuum, or do other chores, make it count. Wait until the carpet really needs it and be proud of those loud, gravelly sucking noises. That means you're using your time to do something that really needs to be done. Smart woman.

Another myth I heard involves bathrooms. A woman giving a home organization seminar recommended you clean a bathroom every time you go into it. This is a seriously bad idea. The bathroom is the *only* place I can go to be alone. If I have to straighten up and clean it whenever I enter, my last refuge is ruined. Ditto the idea of cleaning the shower while you're taking one. I live for showers. Hot, steamy, sound-proof showers are my idea of heaven, and the experience loses something if I have to scrub the tub.

My last housework misconception involves the laundry. A how-to-be-neat book advised me not to start a new load of laundry until I had folded and put away the load that just came out of the dryer. *Never, never do this.* When you do laundry, let everyone—family, friends, neighbors—know you're doing laundry. Proudly fold it and stack it in a prominent place. (I now do it on the couch in front of the window in the living room.) I did this last week and my husband came home and said, "Wow, I can't believe you did all that laundry." I rest my case.

Another laundry tip I recently learned is to call laundry violations. At our house there are just three simple laundry violations: Putting obviously clean clothes in the hamper (if they're folded, it's a dead giveaway); wearing different pajamas every night; and getting a new towel for each shower. I have even given them math problems: If everyone in the family wears different pj's every night, how many pj's will we have to wash each week? The answer is forty-two. All the talking in the world did nothing until I established the

laundry penalty. If you're busted, you put away your laundry plus someone else's.

So there you have it. My crusade has begun. I see my life in a new light. My job is to put housework in its place. We mothers have lots of things to deal with, and housework anxiety should not be one of them.

I read a book years ago that said the cruelest thing a woman can do is to invite a new mother over and have a spotless house, sweet children in matching outfits, and all sorts of homemade goodies. The new mother will feel totally inadequate. I like to think my ministry encourages and builds up other mothers. When women come to my house, they suddenly feel good about themselves and their homemaking abilities. They leave with smiles on their faces.

Making other women feel good this way is not something that all women can or should strive to do, but the payoffs make it worthwhile for me. Just this past year I received a plaque that read, "Clean houses never last... hugs and kisses do."

# The Missing Ingredient
### by Betsy Kilday Crosby

Cook meals in less than thirty minutes! Magazines in the supermarket checkout counter beckon to us with promises of quick dinners and cover pictures of enticing, nutritious meals.

Magazines that promise those quick meals have staffs who prepare them in test kitchens. Test kitchens that are spotless and stocked with state-of-the-art cookware. Test kitchens with time-and-motion experts who faithfully record every move the cook makes.

Test kitchens that have all the right ingredients, but not a basic ingredient found in my real kitchen—children.

Children add spice to our lives and havoc to our kitchens. A time-and-motion expert would have a hard time recording my every move as I made a "thirty-minute or less" lasagna recipe, and here's why.

**Test Kitchen:** Chop onion and sauté until translucent. Brown one pound hamburger meat and drain well.

**Real Kitchen:** Chop onion, halfway. Shut refrigerator door left open by growing son in search of after-school food. Answer front door. Welcome friend Sarah and two of her children. Take seats out of van, load children, go to church and load ten folding tables for a co-op garage sale. Sarah returns home to fetch Little League uniform, leaving two children. All children present stand around in kitchen and then forage in refrigerator for freeze-pops. No one can "Tear here." Use onion-chopping knife to behead freeze-pops. All boys present make karate sounds as I chop. Children banished from the kitchen, leaving door open. Close door. Brown meat. Drain in colander, recently retrieved from sandbox (but washed very, very well).

**Test Kitchen**: This magazine lasagna is featured in a cholesterol-lowering olive oil diet. Olive oil contains a substance that hooks up with bad cholesterol and wisks it through our arteries. Therefore, we can load lots of mozzarella cheese on top of our lasagna and not worry.

Open tomatoes, sauce and pasta; add to the onions and meat. Simmer with fresh Italian spices.

**Real Kitchen:** Our real kitchen lasagna is a featured meal in the *We're Going to Move so We Have to Eat Everything* diet.

There is no nutritional basis for this diet; our goal is simply to eat up everything stored in the garage cabinet. Tonight we'll eat up four cans of tomato sauce. This diet sounds horrendous, but at least we're still on the second cabinet shelf. The first shelf has three cans of clam chowder (supermarket special from two years ago) and seven cans of chicken noodle soup (last flu season).

**Test Kitchen:** Cook lasagna noodles al dente.

**Real Kitchen:** Put on pot of water for noodles. Hear strange sound on the roof. Run outside and almost collide with ladder placed against the house. Find medium-sized boy (extra, from next door) trying to retrieve a badminton birdie from the roof. He is standing on ladder step clearly marked "DANGER: DO NOT STAND ON THIS STEP." Consider wringing all boys' necks, but settle for lecture on safety. All boys present roll their eyes heavenward and promise never, ever to go on the roof again.

Return to kitchen. Mop up overflowing boiling water.

**Test Kitchen:** Mix together one package of thawed and drained spinach with one egg, one cup cottage cheese; $1/4$ cup Parmesan cheese and (hooray!) one tablespoon olive oil.

**Real Kitchen:** Answer door. Welcome Sarah who fetches her son who changes into Little League uniform. She leaves her daughter who joins my daughter to color pictures at the kitchen table in the middle of the spinach, eggs, olive oil and Parmesan cheese.

Mix together above items. Open and quickly discard two mostly empty cartons of unspeakable cottage cheese. Promptly take smelly trash outside. Find another boy setting up the ladder. Lecture loudly. Retrieve two birdies from the roof and put ladder in an impossible-to-reach location. Return to kitchen.

**Test Kitchen:** Grease 9"x13" pan. Spoon meat mixture over bottom; layer with noodles, then spinach mixture, noodles and rest of the meat. Top with lots of grated mozzarella cheese. Bake in 350° oven until brown on top.

**Real Kitchen:** Answer door; greet Sarah. The Little League game was canceled. She collects her daughter and says goodbye. Husband comes home from work, sits at the kitchen table and eats Cheetos.® Son, still growing, forages for more food.

Layer lasagna with interruptions and conversation.

**Test Kitchen:** Serve the lasagna on a clean table set with daisies in a vase, a checkered table cloth and drinks served in coordinated glassware. Take magazine cover picture.

Time elapsed for preparation: thirty minutes.

**Real Kitchen:** Remove from table thirteen crayons, seven papers, one Barbie® doll leg, one badminton racket, two badminton birdies, one Cheetos bag and one hairy hairbrush. Pour milk into plastic glasses. Serve lasagna with a flourish.

Time elapsed for preparation: two hours and forty-seven minutes.

Eat in fifteen minutes.

# Library Phobia

### by Rosemary Raymond Horvath

**I** must be the only mother in America who says, "You're grounded from the library until you're twenty-one."

I know moms who can happily spend the morning at the library while their little angels are sitting and listening to the librarian read stories. Not me. I once had the occasion to remove three children from Story Hour and whisk them off to the bathroom where I could discreetly (I thought) threaten them with loss of life. Wrong. The ventilation system of the library was such that every word was clearly audible where the tittering moms were sitting.

It is not that my children are particularly naughty; on a scale of one to ten (ten being the worst), they are about four. The problem is that I love books and forget to hover around my children at the library. I get sucked into the stacks, where entire worlds await, inviting me on adventures of mind and spirit. I don't even care which aisle I'm in; I can be just as easily enticed by murder mysteries as cookbooks, crafts as high finance. I am like the TV addict who will watch test patterns—any book will do. I have even read my husband's soil pathology books, which is pathological indeed. Even cereal boxes captivate me.

My family shares my addiction. We flop around our living room, everyone with a book, and glorious disarray reigns. I have moments of sheer pleasure just watching my family read; a little music in the background, and I know just what heaven feels like.

There are, however, drawbacks. I got a registered letter in the mail the other day. I thought it was going to be my *Reader's Digest* sweepstakes winning notification, as that is the only registered letter I am looking for. It was, in fact, a letter from the library stating that if I didn't return our overdue books in two weeks, I'd be guilty of a misdemeanor. It seems my twelve-year-old had checked books out on four different cards and lent the books to friends—last summer. The fine came to sixty-six dollars and seventy-five cents. He can't recall to whom he lent the books, and will be working without pay for some time.

I have tried many systems to keep our library books straight. I kept a basket by the front door where all but the currently read books were to be kept. I found socks, Lego® blocks, our own books and my telephone bill in it. I tried making a list of every book brought into the house, who checked it out and when it was due. I entered it in the computer, the day before the head crash wiped out all my computer files. I would have forgotten what it was listed under anyway. I tried limiting the number of books to be checked out. No matter what, we return our public library books to the school and vice versa. But we are not lending them out to friends anymore!

I was mad at my husband the other night and decided to run away from home. Where did I go? To the library. Could I check out books? No, I had no money and my fines had added up again. Things look pretty bleak when you can't afford to go to the library.

But then, at dinner the next night, I listened to the conversation with new ears: there were literary references sprinkled throughout the conversation, and I was delighted with the level of discussion when a child could draw a comparison between a Dickens character and a person in the news. I guess I can call my library budget "tuition." And if the library habit doesn't get under control, it may be the only tuition I'll ever be able to afford!

# About Ladies

I've always thought that "ladies"
Have bee-hive hair-dos
that are stiff with hairspray
wear pink nail polish
on long pointy nails
play bridge
leave lipstick marks on straws
and coffee cups and even sandwiches
not to mention your cheek when they kiss you
have at least fifty pairs of shoes
stacked up in shoeboxes on the closet shelf
wear pantyhose under slacks
have worn out purses
with old yucky make-up old yucky tissues
and lots of other old yucky junk in them
never run always walk
never sit on the floor
go to the beauty parlor every Friday
are scared of spiders garden snakes
and even fireflies
take forever to get ready to go somewhere
do not drink milk

\*    \*    \*

then yesterday I rang a neighbor's bell
and a little boy said
mom there's a lady at the door

*Betsy Statman Besl*

# Alone on Planet Parent

## by Pam Lunardi

It's 6:30 p.m. and my daughters are chasing each other up and down the stairs, shrieking at the tops of their lungs. The house looks as though we have been attacked by aliens. I follow the trail from the kitchen, down the hall and into the living room... books, toys, scattered papers, empty cups, bits of food, discarded clothes. I clear a path to the couch and sit for a minute. My husband is holed up at his office two miles away, where he has spent every spare moment for the past two weeks in preparation for a looming deadline.

He's been leaving in the morning before the girls wake up, and getting home long after we are all asleep. I thought I had been handling this well, but today I think we all went over the edge.

Did I really scream at Emily, "BE QUIET! YOUR SISTER IS SLEEPING!" Did I really stifle her rambling anecdotes about the kids next door in order to rush her into her ballet leotard, only to have her get so upset that she sobbed until she hyperventilated and had to stay home from ballet? Was it during this incident that I reminded her "Nobody's perfect," only to have her reply, "You're not perfect, but Daddy is"?

When I asked, "How many times have I asked you to stop singing 'Twinkle, Twinkle, Little Star'?" did she really look at me seriously and guess, "Thirty?"

Have I been yelling as much as I think I have? Is that why two-year-old Elizabeth tugged on my leg and said, "I sorry, Mommy" when she saw her sister's tears, even though she was in the other room when the crying began? Did I really give them Honey Nut Cheerios® for dinner?

For the moment, they seem content to be cheerfully flinging dolls down the stairs. The kitchen timer goes off. This is to remind me that I promised a friend, a flourishing professional who has no children, that I would call into a local live television show tonight to discuss my impressions of her work while she appears on the show as a guest. Now I am wondering if I made this promise in a moment of insanity. How am I going to talk on the phone, thoughtfully, quietly, for twenty minutes? I'm alone on Planet Parent, with no reinforcements in sight.

There appears to be someone at the door. "Daddy!" the girls shout. Knowing better, I reach for the door handle, feeling sorry for the person who is about to enter this scene of domestic chaos.

It's... it's... my *babysitter*! Suddenly I remember that weeks ago, anticipating a night out with a friend, I had asked if she would come over tonight. I never made those plans, but here she is. My head starts to clear. I can call the television show! She can put them to bed! I can... I can *go somewhere else*!

First, I make the phone call. Next, I decide, I will go to the library and stay there until it closes. The girls are chasing each other again, only this time they're naked.

Coleen is running their bath, and she's laughing as hard as they are.

I close the door behind me and take a deep breath. There is such a thing as serendipity, I think. I will take an hour or so to gather the shreds of my patience, and resolve to act like an adult again. I will apologize to the girls for my grumpiness. I will ask Coleen if she can come again on Thursday! I will speak to my daughters in a reasonable tone of voice and offer lots of hugs and kisses. And in a few more days, Daddy will beam himself down and rescue me from this beleaguered planet.

# Lunch Sneezed

We lie side by side:
You, for a midday meal,
Me, for some much needed rest.
One hand tilts my breast
The way a native woman grasps a gourd
Brimming with nectar.
Your other hand, a darling little sand-crab,
Explores afield,
Collar, neck, nose, hair…
EXPLOSION!
You jerk back and regard me with
Startled eyes,
Mouth stunned into an O.
I smile and pinch your flushed cheek.
"I'm sorry," I giggle.
"Lunch sneezed."

*Joanne Sydney Lessner*

# Martha and Me

### by Francesca Huemer Kelly

**S**he's blonde, creative and terrifyingly capable. Her message is simple: you and I can live just the way she does, if we simply follow the directions in her magazine, ominously titled *Martha Stewart Living*.

Not only is it named for her, but she's almost always on the cover, smiling as she paddles a canoe or makes gingerbread houses for the holidays. And right in the first few pages is her calendar for the month. I guess it's there so we can share Martha's days with her, live her life along with her. We prune our roses on the same day she is pruning hers. We paint our shutters on the same day she paints hers. The photographs are gorgeous, she's gorgeous and the magazine is selling like hotcakes. As a harried, rapidly aging mother of four young children, I understand why people buy it— we all like to dream.

But one day recently when I was perusing my own calendar, I reflected that Martha Stewart's life really isn't so different from mine. She grew up in northern New Jersey; so did I. She likes hanging out in the kitchen; so do I. (So what if she's cooking there and I'm eating there?) If you don't believe me, just listen to these entries from the calendar of *Martha Stewart Living*, compare them to my own calendar entries, and see if we don't have a lot in common:

**March 6**

Martha: Shop for hiking gear for trip to India; break in new boots.

*Me: Trip to the discount shoe store for the entire family! Older kids have tantrums about non-designer shoes; younger kids have tantrums about having to behave in public. Mom remains calm; saves her tantrum for the car ride home.*

**March 7**

Martha: Refinish kitchen cupboards at Turkey Hill.

*Me: Clean out refrigerator to find out what's causing that smell.*

**March 13**

Martha: Subscribe to computer on-line service and establish personal e-mail address.

*Me: Attempt to go on-line. Discover computer has no modem.*

**March 18**

Martha: Order manure delivery for vegetable gardens.

*Me: Watch neighbor's dog "fertilize" my future zucchini patch—again!*

**March 22**

Martha: Appear on "The Today Show."

*Me: Pose for "before" picture at weight loss center.*

**March 27**

Martha: Have East Hampton lawn rolled and re-seeded.

*Me: Give up on saving lawn from crabgrass and tricycle tracks, and investigate blacktopping the entire thing.*

Well, on second thought, maybe we weren't exactly separated at birth. I see that now. Take these friends' and relatives' birthdays and anniversaries on the calendar in the latest issue, for example. Here we see "Charlotte Beers' birthday" written on June 26, and "Laura and Randy's anniversary" on June 28. Who *are* these people? Am I supposed to know? Am I supposed to care? More important, am I supposed to send a card to Charlotte Beers when I can't even remember my own sister's birthday? No, no, of course not, I say reassuringly to myself. Martha's calendar is there just as a model, just as a suggestion of how I could be living my life if I were not, say, overweight and brunette and the mother of four kids.

Still when the latest issue of *Martha Stewart Living* hits the stands, I always seem to buy it—and soon find myself contemplating building a garden shed or force-feeding everyone bouillabaisse. Is it so very bad to play the role of Domestic Goddess, even if it's just for a few days? Probably. Not long ago, after reading an article about setting up a home office using antique farmhouse tables and old rabbit hutches for file cabinets, I went right out and dropped the five hundred dollars I'd saved for a new dental crown on beat-up "primitive" furniture. Somehow it doesn't quite fit in with the juice-stained green vinyl recliner. And I still have a broken back molar.

In fact, Martha's not the only one pushing me to be someone I'm not. There are dozens, even hundreds of magazine articles out there telling me—and lots of other American women—how to live our lives. Evidently we try to do everything they tell us, because there are also plenty of articles out there ordering us to slow down and relax, instead of trying to do it all. "Meditate," they urge us. "Run a bubble bath." Are they kidding? The few times I've tried to meditate, I've fallen asleep, only to be awakened by either the kitchen smoke detector or someone's sticky fingers poking my eyelids. And what mother doesn't long for a bubble bath! In fact, I think I'll go tell my kids to get their own supper, clean up the kitchen, sit right down and merrily do their homework, finish a couple of loads of laundry, then put themselves to bed. "Thanks, kids," I'll say, "if you need me, I'll be in the tub."

But the advice is still flying at us. Check out the covers of most women's magazines. What's with the numbers, anyway? "Twenty-eight Time-Savers You Can't Live Without!" "Thirty-five Ways to Drive Him Wild in Bed!" "Eighteen Cancer-Proofing Foods You Must Eat!" Here's one I'd like to see: "Three Hundred and Two Tiny Bits of Useless Information Designed To Make You Believe That Whatever You Are Doing, It's Not Good Enough!" But I will say one thing for *Martha Stewart Living*: There are no numbers on the cover. Just her. I guess that's intimidating enough.

Back to the bubble bath. The other night I decided a bubble bath sounded like a great idea. I checked my calendar, and it just so happened I had some time free at 2:00 a.m. It wasn't on Martha's calendar but I decided to go ahead anyway, for it had been a very long day and I felt old, tired and ready for the trash heap. I

got out the special *Martha Stewart Living* gardening issue and made sure everyone was sound asleep. Then I ran a hot bath, dumped some bubbles in, lay back in the sudsy water and promptly fell asleep. When I woke up and retrieved Martha, she was one wrinkled, wet dame. Hey, maybe we're more alike than I thought.

in her garage
two new cars
both by Fisher-Price®

*Robert Deluty*

# The Laundry Dance

## by Barb Warner

The laundry dance. I hesitate to write about it, to admit that I have taken part in such a thing. I get courage from the knowledge that I'm not alone. Some of my friends have confessed to me, in weak moments, that they have "done the dance." So I've decided it's time for me to come clean (so to speak) and acknowledge that I, too, know the steps to the laundry dance.

What is it? There are *many* variations, for each person's dance is unique, but basically it goes like this:

It's laundry day so you start out with great motivation and high expectations. You say, "Yes, I'll get twenty-five loads of laundry washed, dried, folded, ironed and put away. Never mind that each load takes forty minutes alone to wash and it's already mid-morning. I can do it." You start admirably enough; promptly emptying the washer, hanging or drying clothes and going through the endless repetitive cycles of it all. But, by mid-afternoon, there have been several of a million possible interruptions (or perhaps just a good book calling your name), and you have slowed down. If you're really driven, you've kept on track and put away each load of clothes before the next is dry. That's the way it *should* be done, and I do that maybe once a year.

But if you're like me, on the other hundred laundry days per year you take the dry clothes, sort them, fold them, and put them in piles (usually on the bed). You start with a pile for each family member (six, in my case), and separate piles for towels, sheets, clothes to be ironed, clothes to be rewashed, stain-treated, or bleached, and of course, a pile of unmatched socks.

You work through the day, and at any one time you will have clothes in piles on the floor waiting to be washed, clothes in the washer, clothes in the dryer, clothes in a basket waiting to be taken upstairs to be put in the piles and the piles themselves. Is any of this familiar to you?

On a good day, you will finish the laundry and the piles will all get put away. The laundry is over, you're on to a new adventure. On a bad day, you won't have finished "the dance" when bedtime rolls around. You'll wait until you're dog-tired and could sleep on a bed of nails, and you'll crawl up to your bed to find... the piles. What will you do? If you're really dog-tired, you won't take all those piles and put them away. No, sir. You might wake the children if you did that (good rationale). No, you will put those piles somewhere else. This is where the dance gets going.

The worst place to put the piles is back into the laundry baskets and/or hampers. Unless you're up at the crack of dawn to finish this mess (and if we were like that we wouldn't have this problem to begin with), you'll be washing clean clothes before the week is up (trust me on this one). Another bad place is the floor around the foot of your bed. It starts your morning off poorly when you kick the piles and have to sort and fold them again. Actually, I don't know where a good spot is; it's a hard call. But you'll find some place for the piles, plop into bed and dream sweet dreams about big laundry rooms and maids.

Then morning comes, and... it's not laundry day anymore. The pressure is off, and you think, "I can just finish this up in between my other chores." You're wrong, but you naively proceed. You take the really wrinkled clothes from the dryer (the ones that sat there all night) and perhaps rewash the smelly clothes that have mildewed in the washer, and you're on your way. Before the first load is ready to sort, however, you get all of your piles out again and put them back on the bed.

By now your dance has probably been complicated by someone who has dug through the piles looking for a favorite shirt, by others who have thrown dirty clothes on top of the clean piles, or just by the fact that you now have enough new dirty clothes for another load of laundry. If you're smart, you'll realize you're on the verge of a really big disaster, cancel all plans for the day, unplug the phone and do laundry. Otherwise, you'll be moving, shuffling and dancing with piles of clean and dirty clothes all week. It won't be pleasant.

Now, that's just one example of how "the dance" can be done. I know people who have moved the same piles of clothes on and off of their beds for close to a week. I walked in on a friend who had accumulated a virtual mountain of clean, wrinkled clothes on her bedroom floor. At the time she had two small children and a newborn, and I assured her that she would *never* get it all folded by herself, so we did it together. I've seen some do "the dance" once a week with huge amounts of clothes, and I've seen others "dance" who do their laundry every day. It doesn't happen all the time to any of us, but if it happens even once, we remember it.

For those of us who want to have everything under control, laundry dancing makes us feel totally disorganized and unable to do a simple chore. It's embarrassing and something we don't like to admit. However, we parents need to know that we're not alone when we get off track. We should step up and confess our laundry sins (and other household and parenting transgressions). I know that I felt so much better when some of my most "together" friends shared their own horrifying laundry stories.

The best one was told by a mom who had been doing "the laundry dance" for quite a while. She came home one day to find her husband had backed his pickup up to the door and was throwing clothes into the bed of the truck. He said, "I hired a baby sitter and we're going to the laundromat. We will never be able to do all this laundry." They used fourteen washers and got caught up. When she admitted this in front of a group of moms, we all laughed until we cried, and then the rest of us spilled our guts.

Confessing to "laundry dancing" was therapeutic, and it brought us closer together. It was good to laugh at ourselves and our laundry and get everything into perspective. Maybe "laundry dancing" isn't so terrible after all.

# We're in This Together

# The Men in My Life

## by Rosemary Conroy Hughes

**M**y children have had several different fathers.

The man who coached me through my first labor and delivery was afraid to move a muscle when the nurse handed him our newborn daughter. But now my kids have a dad who embarrasses them by holding other people's babies every chance he gets.

I remember a fellow who ate hot dogs while our toddler enjoyed rack of lamb (medium rare), because we couldn't afford to buy enough lamb for all three of us. These days, the man we call Daddy eats lentils no matter how many lamb chops I buy; he worries that his cardiovascular system can't afford all that red meat.

It seems as though the trend in our family is towards prudence and sensibility in the dad department. My oldest three remember the time when their dad carried them all upstairs to bed at once, one on his shoulders and one under each arm. My little ones have a dad who does his stair climbing on a machine, and never lifts anything heavier than his back brace.

The father of my two oldest children worked nights and weekends trying to meet his boss's expectations. But he always managed to be there for piano recitals and school plays, even if the boss disapproved. Today the father of my children works nights and weekends because he has to set the standard for his employees. But he always manages to be there for piano recitals

and school plays. He says that's the best example he can offer to the people who work for him.

This more mature father is more casual than when he was younger. He would have rushed his first child to the emergency room when her umbilical cord fell off, but when one of his younger kids crunched a finger in the car door, he gave the boy a cold can of soda to hold, while announcing in a solemn Marcus Welby voice that it didn't look broken to him.

Other times, though, experienced dads can be awfully particular about the little details of parenting. Years ago, this dad figured babies could sleep just as well in a backpack or car seat as they could at home. Now he won't accept invitations that require us to wake the baby up before he's finished his nap.

My sedentary kids are plagued by the dad who insists that they get out and play, for crying out loud. The more active children in our family are persecuted by the dad who wants a little peace and quiet, for pete's sake.

It's been an interesting experience, watching the metamorphosis of my children's father. Sometimes I miss the young guy who could push a stroller uphill all afternoon without tiring. I often wonder what happened to the proud papa who carried a briefcase full of baby pictures that he displayed to friend, foe or stranger at the slightest provocation.

But the man I live with now can spend endless hours showing a baby how to crawl down the stairs safely, and never once lose his patience. He can't al-

ways name the kids whose pictures fatten his wallet, but he remembers all their favorite ice cream flavors and can find their missing shoes in an instant.

The twenty-something fellow who washed every surface of our house with chlorine bleach before his first baby came home from the hospital probably wouldn't recognize the guy who nowadays wipes a dropped pacifier on his shirt before jamming it back into the baby's mouth.

The dad who assembled our crib for the first time wore tapered dress shirts, drove a two-door car and had ambitious plans for his children's futures. But the dad we have today buys relaxed-fit blue jeans, belts two car seats into the back of his station wagon, and gets misty-eyed when he remembers his older children's baby years.

I loved that young father of days gone by, but I'm pretty fond of the grey-haired version, too. Seems like this dad just keeps getting better and better.

# Small Norman

Small Norman has a habit
Of getting up at night
And climbing down the stairs to say
His jammies are too tight,

Or that his ears are burning hot,
Or that his toes are freezing,
Or that he cannot sleep because
His teddy bear keeps sneezing,

Or that he fears a giant may be
Peeking in his window,
Or that he's thirsty—how about
A little cup of cocoa?

His parents don't know what to do
When Norman reappears.
They've pleaded with him, reasoned, and
   yelled,
Yet still—he perseveres!

Each night when they tuck Norman in
And help him say his prayers
They breathe a whispered prayer themselves
That Norm will stay upstairs.

But still he clambers down and up,
His problems to recite:
His sheets are snarled, his fingers itch,
The night-light is too bright.

"Why, Norman, why?" his parents cry.
"Why won't you stay in bed?"
And Norman looks down at the rug
And scratches his small head.

"When I lie down I pop back up
Just like a big balloon.
It could be 'cause my pillow's full
Of fuzzies from the moon.

Or maybe 'cause I think of stuff
Like monsters and big bugs.
Or maybe I'm just lonesome, and
I need some extra hugs."

His parents hug and squeeze him then
And carry him back up.
They bring a drink of water
In a tiny paper cup.

They fluff and smooth his pillow, and
They check him head to foot,
Then tuck him in real tight and murmur,
"Norman, please stay put!"

Then Norman lies in his dark room
And thinks that bed is boring,
But he will go to sleep now,
If that giant will stop snoring.

*Susan McElwain*

# Billable Hours and Sea Monkeys

### by Donna Marcinkowski DeSoto

**Y**ou arrived just after eleven p.m. and the look on your face told me how grueling your day had been. You were determined to tell me all about it. I was determined to distract you.

*Leave it at the office. Take a break. This is your haven, your oasis. Yes, those are still breakfast dishes in the sink, but let me tell you about the sea monkeys! They came!*

Intent on describing, blow by blow, your horrible day, you recounted that the alarm didn't go off, or we didn't hear it or you hit the snooze button one time too many. You had cut your shower short by almost ten minutes. You noticed while getting dressed that both hems were finally falling out of the suit pants you pulled on. You were missing a button on your last clean shirt, and your power tie was determined to pouf out, exposing the red "X" of the discount outlet where I bought it.

*Sea monkeys. Remember how much we loved that name when we saw the magazine ad? They're finally here; the mailman even brought them to the door. He saw that the package was marked "Contents: Sea Monkeys," and he worried that they might be perishable.*

You had to run for a bus that had no air conditioning on this sweltering 96 degree, 96% humidity day. The weatherman reminded us over and over that the

air quality was in the hazardous range. Which one of us said we wanted to live in the Washington, D.C. area, anyway?

*Have you ever seen a real sea monkey? The kids can't wait until they hatch. They checked them every couple of minutes, all day long. They actually believe these things will look just like tiny little monkeys, with cute chimp faces and long, curling tails.*

Your secretary didn't show up again, and the temp they sent you brought along an attitude and her own little TV set to put on her desk.

*So, we read the directions together right after the mailman brought the package. Andy carefully got the glass of water, and he let Aimee help by pouring in the packet of sea monkeys. They were so excited! Maybe they will stop asking us for a dog and a cat for awhile.*

You found out that one of your filings got sent to a client on the opposing side yesterday. "A big no-no," you added for emphasis. You were late getting your billable hours report, so your paycheck didn't come this morning, and how could we be overdrawn again?

*They were only $2.98; that is not what caused our account to be overdrawn. The kids have come up with all kinds of names for their soon-to-hatch pets. We have no idea how many will make it, but we have plenty of names, just in case this is a good bunch. Andy wrote most of them down: Zorbud, Titanic, Fuselage, Violet Chloe. Where did "Violet Chloe" come from? Aimee just wants to name them all "Aimee." What are sea monkeys, do you know?*

You barely had time to go to the bathroom today. The leftovers you "wolfed down" at your desk for lunch spilled and landed on your shirt. You tried, but tomato sauce only gets worse when you rub it with a dry paper towel.

*We have to feed these things some kind of protein out of a packet. But we can't feed it to them until they hatch or it will kill them. How do we tell when they have hatched? These guys are microscopic. But they do come with a Limited Life Insurance Policy!*

The temp lost an important document on the computer that you'd been working on for two weeks. She says *you* lost it. She even told your boss's secretary. Your secretary left a message that she'd be out for the rest of the week. She wondered if you still had a copy of her resume that you could fax to her.

*We watched and watched for something miraculous to happen in that glass of water. Maybe it will happen during the night. The directions say it can take anywhere from four hours to fourteen days, depending on the conditions. The kids were so afraid they'd miss something while they were asleep.*

On your way out of the building tonight, you rode in the elevator with your boss, who mentioned that he was only going out for a quick bite. Another senior attorney on the elevator called you by the *other* Hispanic associate's last name, and said he hasn't seen you around lately. He glanced first at the place where the button was missing, and then at the big orange splotch.

Finally done pacing back and forth in the family room, you head into the kitchen for your reprieve—a

bowl of Cocoa Puffs®. "Okay, okay," you say. "Where is this gimmick you fell for?" You start to mutter again that this has been one of the worst days you've had in a long time.

As I walk into the kitchen, my eyes open wide and I walk right back out. I just don't have the heart to tell you that you've lost another button on your shirt. And that you just drank the sea monkeys.

# How Do I Love Thee? Let Me Lock the Door

### by Heidi Griminger Blanke

**H**aving three young children in the house tends to stifle marital romance. Every now and then, though, my husband and I think we've got the system beat.

Take this morning, for instance. Since I had fallen asleep over my book at nine o'clock the night before, I was awake and raring to go at dawn. I padded around the house for a few minutes, but couldn't think of a quiet activity. Bored, I stood at my bedroom door, staring at my husband, willing him to awaken.

"Done sleeping?" I asked as soon as I saw an eyelid flutter. He moved his head and uttered an enigmatic grunt. I closed and locked the door and cuddled up next to him. Time: 6:15.

My husband and I snuggled close, absorbing warmth from each other. Our smiles faded as we heard repeated soft raps on the door. Time: 6:30.

"I'm going to take a shower," called our fifth grade daughter, "and I need to get some towels from your bathroom."

As she rummaged for the perfect towel, I whispered to my husband, "No problem. She'll be in the shower for at least ten minutes."

Our daughter returned to the hall bathroom and I again closed and locked our door. My husband and I

assumed our pre-interrupted position.

This time there was no knock at the door, just the sound of a doorknob being turned and a voice shouting "Mommy!" Our four-year-old had to go to the bathroom. Time: 6:40.

Our older daughter is still in the shower. My husband offers the toddler a cup of juice or milk to take to her bed. She only wants Kool-Aid® and a temper tantrum ensues. Feet thud in the hall. The wailing has woken our nine-year-old son. He climbs into our bed and throws a pillow over his head. Time: 6:50.

Our oldest child is now out of the shower and in our bathroom looking for a hair brush. She can't find hers.

My husband kisses my neck, slides out of bed, and heads for the shower. A cold one, probably.

I'm still in bed snuggling, but now the male body next to mine is flannel clad and the naked bottom resting against my side belongs to a preschooler. Time: 7:00.

The alarm goes off.

# The Great Applesauce Adventure

### by Barb Warner

**I**t began when our apple tree grew apples—*lots and lots* of apples. Normally that wouldn't be a problem. In years past, when our tree produced sporadically we ate what we could and gave the rest away. But this year we had experienced the loss of our only income (*that* was exciting....) and thought, "Okay, we can preserve these apples and live on them throughout the long, cold winter."

Well, that's not exactly what we thought, but we figured we had all these apples and really shouldn't take free food for granted, so the apple watch began.

My husband, Dean, kept a close eye on the tree to determine the perfect harvest time. Every few days he'd tell me, "Your apples are almost ready." (He called them *my* apples the same way my sister always called the dog *my* dog when it was time to walk him.) Anyway, Dean was so persuasive that I started to believe the apples were my responsibility and went to work figuring out what to do with them.

My first thought was the dehydrator I had gotten the previous year for my birthday. But I discovered two problems with our first test batches. One was that apples take a very long time to dehydrate, and the other was that the kids and I ate each batch just as soon as they

were dried. Seeing as we had hundreds of apples on the tree, I'd be dehydrating day and night for the next decade.

Okay, plan B. I surveyed my "earthier" friends to see what they would do with an apple tree full of ripe Golden Delicious apples. My friends all assured me that I was so fortunate and that, after freezing some apples for pies (Oh, sure...), what I *should* do is make the rest into applesauce.

Hmmmm.... Could I acknowledge that I'd never made applesauce before? Sure, I'd eaten it, but never made it; in fact, I'd never canned anything. Well it wasn't easy, but I admitted my ignorance. Soon we were overrun with jars, lids, rings, a big pressure cooker, a huge ladder and several canning cookbooks.

Unfortunately, none of my helpful friends volunteered to come over and make applesauce for me. I was pretty nervous about the whole project, but everyone assured me it was "really easy." And, they reminded me, I'd be saving money, as if applesauce is a big ticket item on my weekly grocery bill.

Well, with supplies on hand, all we had to do was wait for the apples. We didn't wait long. Before I knew it, my husband and his merry band of apple pickers were climbing the tree and picking the apples. So the next Saturday, officially designated "Applesauce Day," I awoke early and put on my best applesauce-making clothes and went down to the kitchen—where I procrastinated for several hours. Dean finally prodded me into action by starting to peel the first bucket of apples.

I jumped right in. From there we peeled, cored, cooked, smashed, stirred, blended, cleaned jars, poured, sealed and popped those babies right into the pressure cooker.

After a few hours of work, a friend stopped by to see if she could take our kids swimming for the day. I was so thankful that I invited her and her family back to our house for dinner that night. With the kids gone, Dean and I pushed ahead.

We were a finely tuned applesauce-making machine. In the better part of the day, we turned approximately three hundred apples into thirty-eight quarts of delicious, nutritious and *inexpensive* applesauce. We finished with a half hour to spare before the kids and friends were due back from the pool. We were awesome—sticky and hot, but awesome.

Just as I started to clean the kitchen, everyone came clamoring home (early) from the pool. That was okay. Everything was still under control. While the kids played, I cleaned up and my friend sat on a kitchen stool admiring our jars of applesauce. Dean went upstairs to take a well-deserved and much-needed shower.

As I put the remaining apple skins and cores down the garbage disposal, Dean started his shower. Immediately, we heard a funny noise coming from the downstairs bathroom. My friend went in to check and came out screaming.

By the time I got there, the bathroom was covered in several inches of water and apple debris which was pouring out of the toilet and quickly advancing toward the family room. It took but a second to figure out that

the shower had something to do with it, and I calmly dispatched my oldest daughter to "TELL DAD TO TURN OFF THE SHOWER RIGHT NOW!"

She ran her fastest, Dean turned off the water, and the deluge subsided. We started bailing. About then, the doorbell rang, and some people I didn't know very well came into the house. Dean, figuring the crisis was over, turned the shower back on to rinse off. More apples and water poured into the bathroom and family room (and now under the wall into the laundry room), and the screaming started again.

By the time the shower was off for the second time, my friend and I had dissolved into fits of laughter and couldn't stop. The kids kept running to the bathroom and saying, "Oh, gross," and the people who had dropped by took one look around and left—guess they didn't want to help clean up.

My husband came down from his shower and finally understood the magnitude of the problem, although he failed to see the humor. We bailed while he tried to figure out what was going on. After a few minutes, he concluded that we had clogged the sewer line out to the street with the apple cores and peels in the garbage disposal. As a result, whenever we used any water, debris from the sewer line came in through the downstairs toilet.

I have to admit my husband was a prince. He went right to work on the disgusting clog and kept his cool. Well... he did until our three-year-old, who has never flushed the toilet a day in his life, decided to go potty

and flush. At that point, Dean came into the house and said very quietly, "I think you better go out for pizza." So we did, and we stayed out for a very long time.

When we finally returned home, it was dark and Dean was still outside working on the clog, surrounded by two bottles of drain cleaner, a plumbing snake, a garden hose, a couple of flashlights and a very big glass of wine.

After I put the kids to bed, we sat out front under the stars and listened to the sound of water backing up the sewer pipe: Dean with his wine and me with a quart of applesauce and a spoon—I'm a stress eater. Finally, after almost seven hours, the water burped and gurgled, and the clog was gone. Peace was restored.

As we cleaned the sticky apple mess from the kitchen, bathroom, family room and laundry room, we tallied the cost: two bottles of drain cleaner, one bottle of wine, a plumbing snake, pizza for eleven, eight hours of labor to make the applesauce, seven hours to unclog the sewer pipe and another three hours to clean up. Well, let's just say that this Christmas we will be giving away some very expensive applesauce.

# Mood Swing

Every millisecond
of this day
I have waited
for us to be as husband
and wife.

Teeth brushed,
prayers said,
hugs hugged,
the children are nestled.

But in the so
slow-coming darkness,
satin and lace
instantly
morph to flannel
with three words:
Mommy! A monster!

*Donna Marcinkowski DeSoto*

# Family Dinner

## by Sara L. Smith

**M**y sons are already home from high school when I return from the grocery store.

"Got anything good?" John asks me, peering into the bags. *Good* to John means loaded with sugar, salt or fat.

"A marble cake mix."

Aaron hangs up the telephone and pulls a box of cereal from one of the bags.

"There are more groceries in the car," I announce.

Both boys head out the door, shoving and bickering. At seventeen and fifteen, they're nearly full-grown—now if only their behavior would catch up to their size.

I take a large beef roast from one of the bags. Bottom rounds are on sale this week, and pot roast is a special treat.

In past years, I routinely prepared a nice meal for dinner, the only time of day when our family of seven was all together. Gradually, though, that time has been eroding. At least one of us is absent from the table nearly every night. My part-time job as a school cafeteria worker has depleted my enthusiasm for cooking at home. We've been eating a lot of soup and sandwiches lately.

But tonight is going to be like old times. I'm almost positive everyone will be home. I set seven large potatoes on the counter.

The boys jostle their way back into the kitchen with the rest of the groceries. Aaron shoves three gallons of milk into the refrigerator, breaks two bananas from the bunch and pours himself a bowl of cereal.

"What's for dinner?" John asks me suspiciously while I slice onions over the meat.

"Pot roast, baked potatoes, carrots, salad and cake."

"Do you have to put disgusting onions on the meat?"

"That's the way Dad likes it."

"What kind of icing for the cake?"

"I thought I'd make peanut butter."

"Again? I hate peanut butter icing."

Laura arrives home from middle school. Simultaneously, the telephone rings. "Is Laura there?" inquires a voice of indeterminate gender.

I give her the phone.

"Bye, Mom," Aaron says.

"Wait a minute," I call. "Where are you going?"

"Work. I'll be home at nine."

"But I thought you were off today."

"This is my Friday to work."

I put one of the potatoes back.

"Can't we have pizza?" Laura asks.

"You had pizza for school lunch," I remind her. "I scraped cheese off hundreds of trays."

Laura giggles. "I could eat pizza three times a day."

The telephone rings. It's a girl for Aaron. Laura takes the message.

Twenty-year-old Dana arrives with her sister, Karen, who is ten. "Dana gave me a ride home from school," Karen says, her voice swelling with importance.

"I picked her up about a block from home," Dana explains.

The telephone rings. "It's Christina." Dana hands the receiver to Laura.

"You're home from work early, aren't you?" I ask Dana.

"A little." She inhales the aroma of roasting meat and onions that is permeating the kitchen. "Something smells good."

I recite the dinner menu once again.

"Dave and I are going out to eat," Dana informs me. "Then we'll probably see a movie. We both got paid today." I put another potato back.

"Can I help you make the cake?" Karen asks.

"Sure."

"Mom, may I go to Christina's house?" Laura asks.

"I guess so," I answer. "Be home at six."

Karen and I work together to mix the batter and pour it into the pan. I set the oven timer and head out to the garden to get enough fresh lettuce for salad. The telephone rings again.

"Mom," John calls from the kitchen window, "may I go to the athletic club with Jerry?"

"What time would you get home?"

A pause while John asks for the information. "Eleven. Jerry wants to know if I can spend the night."

"All right," I agree, sighing.

Back in the house, I put another potato back. The cake is done, and I set it aside to cool while I mix the icing.

"Couldn't we have mashed potatoes instead of baked?" Karen coaxes.

"Well... " I prefer mashed myself, and I'll have plenty of gravy. Now that our numbers are down to four, it wouldn't be that much more work. "No," I decide, "Dad likes baked."

I wash the lettuce carefully. One little bug and the kids won't touch garden lettuce all year. The telephone rings again.

"Mom, it's my coach," Karen says.

"We're having a make-up game this evening," the softball coach tells me. I groan.

"Sorry about the short notice, but I really need Karen tonight," he goes on. "Can you have her at the field by 5:30?"

"She'll be there," I say without enthusiasm. I put another potato back.

"You'll have to get your uniform out of the laundry hamper," I tell Karen. "I'll fix you a toasted cheese sandwich."

The doorbell chimes while I'm making the sandwich. It's Dave, Dana's boyfriend. "What time will you be home?" I ask Dana.

"Late."

Dana has long outgrown a curfew, but I haven't quite outgrown worrying.

I scrape carrots to put in with the meat. The telephone rings.

"Could you please tell Aaron that Jenny called?" asks a soft, feminine voice.

I add the note to Aaron's other messages: *Heather called, Melissa called, Amy called, Lisa called.*

"I'm ready," Karen announces.

I look at her. "Wash your face. Go to the bathroom. Get your hat. And where's your glove?"

The telephone rings. It's Laura.

"Mom, could I please eat dinner with Christina?"

"But I made a cake," I protest feebly. "Maybe Christina would like to eat over here."

"Please, please," Laura begs, "they're ordering a pizza."

"All right," I snap, "be home at eight."

I put another potato back. Then I wrap the remaining two potatoes with foil and set them in the oven. I arrange the carrots around the meat. The roast is browning nicely and smells delicious, but I seem to have lost my appetite.

I drive Karen across town to the ball field, sulking the whole way. So much for my nice family dinner. Although it's frustrating and discouraging for me, the children's worlds have been expanding for some time. Their commitments now extend beyond the family to include friends, coaches and employers. A nice family dinner was my plan, not theirs.

Ron is home from work when I get back to the house. "Where is everybody?" he asks.

"Dana had a date, Aaron is working, John went to the club with Jerry, Laura is eating with Christina and Karen had a make-up game."

"So it's just the two of us for dinner?" Ron gives me a wicked grin. I smile halfheartedly. "I told Karen we'd come to the ball field later."

"What smells so good?"

"Pot roast and carrots."

"Mmmm. You put onions on top?"

"Sure."

"And baked potatoes?"

"Yep. And salad and marble cake." By now my grin feels genuine too.

"With that good icing I like?"

"Naturally." I start into the kitchen, but Ron stops me, catching me in a big hug and kiss.

"So you made this nice meal just for me?"

I hug him back. "Of course."

# My Wife's Night Out

## by Samuel P. Clark

**B**aby clothes are usually defined by a series of snaps and buttons down there where it really matters, the complexity of which is certainly the maniacal creation of some displaced NASA engineer. (This technical misfit is still holding a major grudge because his pet project—to determine whether crunchy peanut butter retains its crunch in a state of weightlessness—got canceled.) If you have not calculated every angle of the fitting and re-entry trajectory to the manufacturer's exact specifications for reattachment, then the vault won't close and what you're trying to protect stays in the sunshine.

But putting Kayla back together after a change is just one of many challenges I am contemplating as I listen to the fading sputters of my wife's '87 Hyundai speeding from our driveway. This is her night out, and she isn't wasting a second of it. I am now officially the babysitter. My wife hates it when I refer to spending time alone with our nine-month-old daughter as "babysitting." She thinks I should refer to it as "parenting."

My argument is that my only experience with parenting was when I had one of those miniature turtles as a kid. In spite of my guidance and devotion, after about three weeks its shell grew really soft, and one morning when I went to sprinkle food in its water, my turtle was belly-up in the pool. Parenting feels too intricate for

what I do. April's counterpoint involves words such as "learn" and "responsibility" and probably makes a lot of sense, but the pitch in Kayla's voice tells me I gotta go...

And I do a lot according to Kayla's pitch. Like this morning, when I got up very early because she was crying at sunrise. I scooped her from her crib and we snuggled in the rocking chair as I listened to her go through her da-da-da-ya chant. Now, I'm no linguist, but it's pretty evident to me that this little song really goes Dad-Dad-Dad-Yea! At least when we do our duet that's the part I sing. During quiet times like these, I often close my eyes so I can totally focus on the sweet softness of her voice. I want to hold her sound in my heart forever.

But now a different noise from the bedroom jolts me to my present reality. That clank merits investigation, and Kayla is shrieking like a siren from a fire truck. I gotta go...

As soon as I come into Kayla's view, she adjusts her shrill cries to a babble and gives me a toothless grin. Feeling reassured, she decides it is a good time to do some cleaning. Kayla doesn't like to have anything on her shelves. She seems to think that books and toys and games all lined up in orderly rows on bookcases detract from the natural grainy wood luster of the shelves. So one by one, or occasionally by a quick sweep of an arm, each blighting object is removed and tossed randomly on the floor. I leave her there, content in her work, and go nab myself a little slice of cake. It's odd to me, but Kayla's view of floors is just the opposite of her posi-

tion regarding shelves. The more obstacles for her to wade through the happier she is. Lemon cake is my favorite, and I hope that before the night is over I'll finish this piece, but at this particular moment, I notice something out of the corner of my eye crawling toward me in the dining room, out of sight under the table, fingers outstretched on my leg, a mouth on my knee. So I gotta go...

Kayla reaches with her right hand and grabs hold of the index finger on my left hand. In order for us to attain the mobility she desires, I must bend toward her like an arthritic old man. When I do she takes off with the fervor of a filly at the Kentucky Derby. We walk and walk everywhere, back and forth; her pitch is excited and my side hurts a little. I put her in the backpack (which she graciously allows me to do) and I begin some chores. Pick up Pooh, Curious George, rattles and blocks. Do dishes. I think I'll vacuum, but Kayla thinks I won't; she wants off my back. I love her timing.

"You explain it to your mom," I say.

She responds with a noncommittal yawn.

"Let's watch TV," I suggest.

A body stretch, accompanied by a deeper yawn, is her reply.

So I take a bottle and about half the stuff I just got from the floor to entertain her in case the show fails to fascinate, and we march off to the TV room. Each toy in turn is studied, tasted, swung around carelessly and inevitably discarded over the arm of the chair. When I'm down to less than five squirmy seconds per toy, I

know I am in trouble. Lacking any foreseeable alternative, I reluctantly reach over to the lamp stand and hand over to her the power of man: the remote control. It is immediately evident that the significance of this gesture is not lost on her. She sits up in my lap, examining the black box with both her hands. At first her fingers move tentatively over the buttons, then with increasing familiarity. With a sigh and a grunt, she tosses the remote over her shoulder and it crashes on the carpet. So much for gifts passed from fathers to daughters.

I resort now to the nectar extracted earlier in the day from mother for daughter by a weird plastic device that frankly makes me squeamish. Kayla appears to take no offense at the methodology used to prepare her meal, and grabs at the bottle with the enthusiasm of a Sumo wrestler who has just ended a forty-day fast. I rock gently as she sucks, and think of my lemon cake.

In another ten minutes, my baby Kayla is snoring undaintily in my arms and I am just a moment's walk from her crib, a glass of milk and a fork. I gotta go...

# The Yellow Bathroom

## by Barb Warner

**T**here was once a Mom who liked to plan. Although she was not what you'd call an organized person, she planned things far in advance. She just liked planning. She enjoyed thinking about what she would do in the future. Sometimes this was a good thing; sometimes it wasn't.

Now this Mom had a small, dingy bathroom. It was beige and drab and hadn't been spruced up for at least ten years. The mom had noticed the sad state of the bathroom and for about six months had been planning to fix it up. There was some leftover white paint in the garage, just enough for this tiny bathroom. There was an attractive blue and white striped shower curtain at a store in town that she had been keeping her eye on (blue being her favorite color and the color of the bathroom carpet). The Mom had it all worked out.

She mentioned her plan to the Dad early one Sunday morning. She told him she was going to paint the bathroom. He perked up. "Oh good," he said, "it really needs it." Then he replied, "What color?" As mom laid out "the plan" before him, she could see he wasn't listening too carefully. "White," he said. "Bright white? Oh no! It will look too stark. That bathroom is too small for white. That white paint in the garage? No, no, no, that will never work."

Now this bothered Mom, but she prided herself on being easygoing (at least other people said she was) and she was willing to compromise. "Okay," she replied, "an off-white would be fine. You may pick it out, since we don't have any paint that color."

Mom was feeling especially pleased with herself. She had not made a big deal over a particular shade of white. She was being quite flexible and so mature. And besides, she really didn't think that Dad would bother to drive to the hardware store to look at white paint.

Mom was wrong. Not only did Dad go to the store and look at white paint, he looked at other colors as well. Yellow colors. Mom, it could be said, just about hated yellow. There was probably nothing yellow in her whole house. Dad, however, was taken by a shade of yellow called "Arctic Spring." He came home with this custom-mixed paint, a new roller and a new rolling pan. He was ready for Mom to paint.

Mom, however, was not ready to paint anything yellow—especially *this* yellow. This was not a delicate, soft, summer yellow. It was a screaming yellow—and it almost had a hint of green in it! Mom let Dad know with her tone and lifted eyebrows that *this* yellow was not welcome in her home. Although Mom tried to pretend that nothing was wrong, she was angry that Dad had bought yellow paint when he knew she wanted white. Dad, perceptive fellow that he is, picked up on this thinly veiled hostility. Tensions mounted in the usually peaceful home.

Dad left for work the following day, hopeful that Mom would learn to love yellow or at least live with it. On his return, he ran up the stairs to see what progress had been made in the bathroom. One side of the one small wall had been taped—that was it. Mom was stonewalling.

Mom hemmed and hawed, but finally made her point. Since she didn't like this yellow, she was in no hurry to cover her walls with it. Mom knew this wasn't a good attitude, and she was trying to change it, but inside she was still angry about the yellow. Tensions continued to mount.

The next glorious morning, Dad awoke ready to tackle the bathroom himself. To his credit, he taped, painted, cleaned the bathtub and decided to replace the ceiling exhaust fan that hadn't worked in several years. Mom worked downstairs and avoided anything to do with the project for as long as she could.

It was the exhaust fan that finally did them both in. The old fan was hard to remove, and the new fan was tricky to put in and had to be done partially through the attic. When all was said and done, the wires from the old fan were one inch too short to connect the new fan and have it lay flat in the ceiling.

There was much moaning in the yellow bathroom that day. There was also much moaning in the attic that day. Gaping holes were discovered in the roof that had never been seen before; exposed nails above the bathroom ceiling poked Dad continuously while he worked; an exhaust flap and a light fixture were broken that

day. It was not a good day for Dad in the yellow bathroom.

It was not a particularly good day for Mom either. She eventually had to stop hiding downstairs and hold the flashlight for Dad and listen to the yelling. And although she understood Dad's frustrations and felt sorry for him, deep down she really thought he deserved it. She knew her attitude wasn't helping the situation and was trying to change it, but she was still angry—and Dad knew it. The wise children played quietly in their rooms. Another tense day passed.

When morning came again to this once happy home, Mom left her cares, children, husband and yellow bathroom behind and set out for a long, peaceful walk. Taking a long walk was one of her favorite things to do. As she walked, she thought and pondered life—and eventually zeroed in on the yellow bathroom.

*How could he?* she fumed inwardly. *How ugly!* she thought to herself.

*How petty,* a small voice whispered.

*How will I ever find a shower curtain to match that hideous color?* she griped.

*How insignificant,* the voice continued.

Mom tried to justify her opinion—but only for a few moments. She knew the voice and knew it was futile to argue. It was time to listen. She quieted her angry spirit and was flooded with memories of the Dad letting her have her way. She was reminded of people she had met who would love to have a bathroom, a husband or a

home filled with laughter. She thought about the energy she was spending on this trivial matter. She was letting her anger invade her thoughts and was sharing her bad mood with all those around her. She knew she was wasting valuable family time—three days' worth so far—being a crab.

Now it would be great to say that the Mom finished her walk, returned home with her new attitude, looked at the bathroom and it had mellowed into a soft, inviting color. But that didn't happen. It would also be great to say that when Mom came home Dad got down on his knees, repented of his sin of yellowness, offered to repaint and was forgiven. But that didn't happen either. It would be cool to say that Mom went out and accessorized the bathroom with so much style that you barely noticed the screaming yellow. But in a tiny, tiny bathroom, it's hard to hide that kind of color, and Mom is just not that talented.

What did happen is that Mom got a shower curtain—not the neat, blue-striped one, but a filmy yellow and green one. And it looked okay (although it still didn't match the blue carpet). She dug out an old Picasso print which was matted in yellow and hung it in the bathroom (Picasso would be so pleased). In her closet, Mom found a basket her sister had given her with some green in it. It was emptied out, filled with some bath supplies and placed on the toilet tank. Then in what can only be considered as a divinely inspired act, she shampooed the bathroom carpet and the rest of the attached bedroom carpet. She then dusted and generally declut-

tered. In fact, Mom became a cleaning maniac. Flat surfaces were seen that had not been visible for months.

Hearing the commotion upstairs, the rest of the family wisely stayed away. What was Mom doing? Had she cracked under the tension? Was she trashing the place? Eventually when they could contain their curiosity no longer, they crept up the stairs to see what was going on. They peered into the room, not quite sure what they'd find. Trying to read Mom's mood, a few of the brave ones actually came inside and looked around. The second oldest daughter even ventured into the bathroom. She quietly looked around, took it all in and said tentatively, "I don't know, Mom, but I might like it."

That was as much of a stamp of approval as the bathroom ever got. And now, months later, the Mom is still pondering the lesson of the yellow bathroom. She's decided that the bathroom has great parallels to her life: It is far from perfect (the room is still very yellow); it has great, unrealized potential (it could be blue and white); and the people involved have shaped what it is today (her husband, Picasso, her sister and K-Mart). More than that, she's realized that if you take the time to take care of it and clean it up—it's okay. It's even better than okay. It's home.

# Someday
# We'll
# Laugh

# The Move

## by Lori Odhner

**I** assure you that I had done my relocation home-work. For weeks I had methodically packed one hundred and forty-seven boxes, numbered and labeled in eleven different categories. Postcards had been sent to various periodicals and friends to inform them of our move from Albuquerque to pastor a church in the Los Angeles area. Weeks ahead of time I had reserved a room in a hotel in anticipation of a crowded Fourth of July weekend at the Grand Canyon. Each family member had a neatly packed bag for the upcoming three-day trip. I even had a journal ready to record our adventures for the benefit of the children.

In retrospect, though, I can see signs, warnings that I ignored. The first one came when I tried to get the air conditioning in the car fixed just prior to our departure. It was the last week in June, and the temperature already was an embarrassing golf score. All of the service stations responded with a variation of "You want it fixed when?"

An even more jarring alarm sounded when my husband misplaced his driver's license the day before we were to pick up the U-Haul truck. Undaunted, we rented it on my license and signed various documents to the effect that I would be the sole driver, knowing that we would trade places as soon as we rounded the corner.

A final note of alarm sounded when they did not have the trailer hitch we had reserved. Unfortunately, the combined ages of our children did not qualify them for a learner's permit to drive our second car, so we unhitched it and left it with a friend to sell.

Finally, after a flurry of goodbyes and an abbreviated night's sleep, we launched our car-truck caravan. When we arrived in Flagstaff, six hours and thirty degrees later, our first objective was to check into our hotel room. Hot and grumpy, we anticipated a frolic in the pool before trekking over to the canyon. John went into the lobby while I changed a diaper, nursed the baby and tried to restore order to the two vehicles. When he came back out, he didn't look happy. (Not that one can expect lighthearted glee from a man who has driven three hundred and fifty miles with two revolving children in a U-Haul.)

"They won't let six people stay in one room," he grumbled.

"What?" I gasped. Our youngest weighed less than a suitcase, I reasoned. Why would they care?

"Regulations." John parroted back what the desk clerk obviously had expected to be a conclusive argument.

I crumpled up on the curb and began to sob. "I can't take any more," I sniffed. The children stopped fighting to comfort me. We were frying in the parking lot. We were between two homes. The door behind us had already closed; the one ahead of us had yet to open.

At that moment the desk clerk felt compassion for us and came out to tell us she would overlook the rule about room capacity. Rescued from my despair, I dried my eyes, thanked her and gathered my brood. We took enough things for the night into our room while the children explored the ice machine, remote control and little soaps.

"Thanks for staying calm," I said to John.

"Thanks for not staying calm," he replied.

We all had a refreshing swim and a late lunch in the restaurant. I enjoyed my hot tuna melt and wrote a few lines in the kids' journal while they shot straws and kicked each other under the table.

By the time we were winding our way along the last few miles between our hotel and the Grand Canyon, I was beginning to feel sluggish. I had a personal responsibility to appreciate this landmark, however, so I didn't complain. We mingled among the throngs of hikers, photographers and vacationers at the rim of the deepest hole on earth, but all I could think about was how much I wanted to sit down. John counted the kids as they darted from lookout to lookout, and I lagged farther and farther behind.

By evening I was convinced that I was a victim of tuna past its prime, and I steeled myself for a long night. By 2 a.m., I felt so awful that John decided to peel the kids out of bed and race to the emergency room.

What life was like for my husband and children after that I can only guess. I was poked, X-rayed and mulled over by various white-coated strangers, who in short order wheeled me into the operating room. I had an appendectomy.

Poor John was left in limbo with not enough clothes, not enough answers and not enough phone numbers. Somehow he muddled through and took care of four children under less than ideal circumstances. I awoke through an incredibly dense fog of anesthesia to the jostle of my children and the weary smile of my husband.

"Are you OK?" he asked.

"Are you OK?" I asked.

"I called your parents and the insurance. Everything's all right." Today was July 3. My pains had started July 2. Our insurance had begun July 1. "The Lord took care of us."

"I'm grateful," I answered.

As for the truck which was so heavy it actually was leaving ruts in the hotel parking lot, a parishioner from our new congregation flew out to drive it the rest of the way to Los Angeles. People we hardly knew unloaded the furniture and the one hundred and forty-seven boxes. They returned the truck on time, somehow explaining who was driving it and why.

Meanwhile, John and the kids camped out in the hotel room, watched TV and ate. (I'm sure that the condition of the room was gossiped about by maid service.) They came by twice a day to see me, and John asked me when I would be strong enough to travel.

By the fourth day, I was able to hobble to the now-ransacked car, and we checked out of the hospital and the hotel. Now imagine, if you can, the response of four children who have been deprived of their mother's attention for the better part of a week. Picture a toddler, accustomed to frequent nursing, who has been obliged to curb that pleasant activity abruptly and is eager to make up for lost time. Last of all, imagine a mother, acclimated to a cool and comfortable hospital bed and bearing a fragile incision on her abdomen, being thrust into triple-digit heat and the eight eager arms of her children.

As we drove through Needles, I remember thinking about the pioneers who had gone before me. It was so hot that when we closed up the car to run into McDonald's for an ice cream cone, a bottle of juice left in the car burst before we got back.

"People did this in wagon trains without air conditioning," I called to John above the uproar.

"A lot of them died," he called back.

Somehow we did make it through, and when we arrived at our new home we unlocked the front door to find the living room filled floor to ceiling with boxes. The kids ran the obstacle course to check out their new rooms, and I remembered the doctor's instructions: "Get plenty of rest. Don't lift anything."

# Guaranteed!

Unpack all the groceries,
Collapse in my seat;
teen wanders through,
"There's nothing to eat!"

*Gayle Urban*

# Name Calling

### by M. Regina Cram

**W**hen I promised to love, honor and cherish for better or for worse, no one told me about naming the baby. My husband and I suffer from a common marital ailment: Incompatibility. A look inside our closets best reveals our personalities. Peter's closet is lined with "semi-dirty" socks (What, may I ask, is semi-dirty?), clothes worn twenty years ago and items which somehow lost their way *en route* to the hamper. His gravestone surely will read, "You never know when it might come in handy."

In contrast, my motto is, "If it doesn't move within twenty minutes, throw it out." We once had a neighbor who arranged his shirts in alphabetical order by color. While I am not quite that compulsive, I do thrive on law and order. It is a wonder that our marriage survives.

Given our basic incompatibility, I should have anticipated that naming our children would be impossible. His family relies heavily upon lineage; my family has so many fruitcakes that we try to avoid most family names. Peter likes traditional names (read "dull"); I prefer unusual ones. At this writing, we have only weeks remaining to agree upon a name for our third child, and, unfortunately, the task does not get any easier.

For a boy, we began with the traditional look at fathers' and grandfathers' names. That yielded Wilbert,

Harkness and Sidney, among others. So much for that idea. Ancestors offer us totally unwieldy names like Jehosophat and Ebeneezer, or ones which are disastrous with Cram, such as Samuel. Would you send a child into a schoolyard with the name Sam Cram?

We have poured through books of names, genealogy charts, war memorials and Bible stories. One day I scoured the credits at the end of a cartoon to get ideas. But the conversation is always the same. My husband doesn't want "Colin." I don't want "Jon." He doesn't like "Caleb." I know too many Michaels. He knew an obnoxious kid named Owen, but had a terrific friend named Buttons. The only Buttons I ever knew was a neighborhood dog who chewed my favorite stuffed lamb when I was six years old. And so it goes....

Of course, other factors beyond personal preference come into play. The relatives become increasingly vocal with each pregnancy, realizing that this may be the last chance to name a child after Uncle Melville or Great Aunt Bertha. Our four-year-old has suggested the name "Poochie"; the two-year-old prefers to name the child Meredith, in honor of herself. Only our dearest friends offer us the consolation that no one ever registered for junior high with the name Baby Cram.

So, night after night, the negotiations continue. Always the planner, I grow increasingly anxious as the days pass. On the very day that I made a packing list for my hospital stay, Peter said that he had little motivation to settle the issue because the discussion was too theoretical. I suggested that perhaps if my contractions were two minutes apart, he might feel more of an incentive. It is apparent that even our four-year-old is aware of our growing desperation, because yesterday he offered to let us use the name of his bear, Big Teddy. When Peter asked how we could distinguish between the two, Skip was appalled at his ignorance. "Daddy," he sighed, "The one with the fur will be the teddy. The one without the fur will be the baby!"

All the while, it grows increasingly likely that soon we will announce to the world a Pam or Sam Cram.

*We are relieved to say that negotiations were successfully concluded and the Crams welcomed Elizabeth Tierney into their family.*

## Greatest Gifts

Freedom and toddlers
Exact the same noble price:
Ceaseless vigilance.

*Robert Deluty*

# Smiley Faces

### by Maureen Keliher Wade

Colleen offered the rock to me, her plump, little hand held open. "Mommy, this rock writes on cars," she proclaimed. I eyed the rock suspiciously. It was a fist-sized chunk of gravel with a jagged edge chosen from the gravel parking lot where we stood. "You didn't write on the van, did you?" I asked, anxiously looking her in the eye. "Noooo... " my four-year-old daughter responded, her gaze holding mine unwaveringly. "Good!" I said, turning back to help her sisters out of the car. *Chill out*, I thought to myself, *don't always expect the worst from her.*

The day had not been going as I'd planned, and I felt myself slipping into a bad mood. I had convinced my seven-year-old daughter that it would be lots more fun to spend her school holiday with me and her little sisters than to go to a Spanish Club meeting with her friends. So far I was having a hard time keeping that promise.

The lunch at the restaurant had started out fine but quickly took a death spiral when the waitress forgot us. My two-year-old was tired of sitting still, so instead of ice cream after our hamburgers, we all screamed (literally). I screamed at the kids; the baby screamed with fatigue; and the other two screamed for their lost treat. Our after-lunch outing to a nearby historic park looked like it would be a washout too as I raced to get there ahead of the rain. Now that the rain seemed to be holding off, the last thing I needed was Colleen scratching the van with a rock.

I finally got coats on all three girls, and we headed out to enjoy the fall colors, climb trees and explore the gardens of the old plantation. My spirits lifted as the girls ran around and eagerly posed for pictures.

I let the girls run themselves out and then we plopped down next to the fountain to watch the golden fish. My daughters' happy, relaxed faces told me that all three of them were content. I savored the moment. More often than not, the girls are upset with each other over something, and more often than not, the child upset is Colleen. Colleen always seems to be crying about a real or imagined slight from her older sister, or fuming over some transgression perpetrated on herself or her things by her little sister. She is not the type to overlook the small stuff. Her emotions are always running full-tilt, either super high or lowest low.

It doesn't stop with sibling rivalry though. Nothing I do for her is enough. Mothering her requires all my attention and more. She needs me more than her sisters do. When she feels she is not getting her fair share of mom, Colleen lets me know... by talking incessantly, hanging on me when I'm on the phone, slamming doors, screaming... all sorts of creative attention-getters. It seems that no matter how much love and time I give to her, she needs more. I try so hard with Colleen but her demand for me is insatiable. This middle child makes me feel incompetent and frustrated. Most days I never seem to be able to make her happy or even content. So as I sat by the goldfish pond, I smiled. Even Colleen was satisfied today.

The sky darkened and the fall breeze turned into a bracing wind. It was time to drive home. We walked together back to the parking lot and from ten yards away I saw it... or maybe I should say them. Etched on the driver's side of our one-year-old, still-like-new, forest green van were several basketball-size smiley faces. Colleen had been right. That rock did write on cars.

I could not believe what I was seeing. I ran to the van and tried to wipe off what I knew would not wipe off. I considered bellowing out a primal scream; I considered reform school for Colleen. I decided a controlled response would convey my anger in a mature, responsible way, but what actually came out was an incoherent torrent of crazed emotion. It was something like, "You ruined my van... how will I ever explain this to Daddy... you've really done it this time, Colleen... do you know how much money this is going to cost?"

We drove home in deafening silence. The toddler, for once, fell asleep in her carseat, and the other two sat in dread wondering if Mom was really going to lose it when they got home. As I drove, my mind raced. Where was the money going to come from for this? How would it affect our already tight Christmas budget? Would my husband blame me for not watching our wild child more closely? Would our insurance cover this? And what the heck was I going to do with Colleen? She had written on walls before, bitten the baby, and drawn red magic marker spots on her face, but nothing of this financial magnitude. I knew in my heart she had not acted maliciously, but still... this was a big one.

In desperation, I sent Colleen to her room until "Dad got home." An hour would allow me to cool off, make some phone calls, and maybe give her time to nap. I called my husband; I called the leasing agent; I called the insurance claims adjuster. And they all had the same reaction: they laughed. I couldn't believe it. Here I was distraught and everyone was laughing at the thought of six smiley faces on my van!

I spent the rest of the hour thinking about Colleen and my reactions to her. In trying to understand Colleen, I've read all the parenting books, I've consulted the pediatrician, I've talked to my "experts" (the grandparents), and tested out every discipline method available. Three years of "terrible two behavior" had worn me down. And possibly, I'd become so conditioned to formulating a battle strategy to win this child's good behavior that I'd lost my sense of humor. Not that causing $482 worth of damage to the family's main mode of transportation should be encouraged, but a four-year-old drawing smiley faces to decorate her mommy's van is touching and, yes, even funny.

In the end, my husband and I had a serious talk with Colleen about the right places to draw and the less-than-desirable canvasses. We let her know that lying about something you have done wrong just makes things worse when the truth is found out, and we took away some privileges. But we also told her how much we love her and that no matter what she did, we always would.

I've started calling her Curious George, after the children's books about the curious, but very lovable, monkey who is always getting into trouble. And I've learned that a little humor can turn around everyone's mood and salvage a situation that's heading for disaster. No, it doesn't work every time, and Colleen has not become an angel. But I have adjusted my perspective.

And since that day, I've tried to see the lighter side in her mischief a little more often. I've tried hard to give her as many smiles as stern reminders. And I've tried to see that the side of a green minivan can look very much like a chalkboard to a four-year-old with a rock.

## Never Fails!

Little one falls
and skins his knee—
but it doesn't hurt
'til he spots me!

*Gayle Urban*

# The Floor

## by Barb Warner

**W**hen we moved in, the floor was covered by rust-colored carpet. Faded, stained, ugly, old carpet. The previous owners had never moved their furniture and in over ten years the sun had dramatically altered the color of all exposed carpet. It made an interesting pattern on the floor (and helped us decide where to place our furniture). Some areas near the west-facing windows were so faded they had a green tinge to them. It was not pretty. After a few years with our family, the carpet was even worse. Babies had spit up on it, someone who wishes to remain anonymous had tried to clean a "pet stain" with Drano® (don't try that at home...) and there were a million dried Play-Doh® specks we were always trying to pick out of it. It was in very sad shape.

Then my problems were over. A big tax refund was coming and we were going to replace the carpet. The possibilities were endless. No dark colors, we didn't want dust showing up too easily or that fading problem. Not too light of a color—unless we matched it exactly to the color of the dirt in our yard. I studied the problem for weeks; I consulted the experts. My husband didn't care, so the decision was left to me. The perfect carpet would be multi-level, so we could cut chewing gum out of it if necessary, and multi-colored, so it wouldn't show dust, dirt or most juice stains. I was prepared—until I went to the carpet store.

107

The choices overwhelmed me. That is my only excuse. I lost my mind and ordered "ice blue" carpet. One level, one color. But it was a beautiful color. When it was installed my husband thought it looked like the ocean. My friends thought it "opened up the rooms," "brightened up the house," "made everything look larger," "cleaner," "brand new." The compliments went on and on. Oh, what a carpet...for about one week.

After a week or so, the stains started appearing. Small things: a single drip from an orange popsicle, a marker landing point down, a lone raisin stepped on and crushed. But hey, no problem for me. I had my spray-top bottle of carpet cleaner and I was right there, cleaning up behind everyone. I was going to keep that carpet spotless. After a month, larger stains started appearing: a whole glass of apple juice spilled in the family room, a friend's child threw up, finger paints, the list goes on and on. Even the dog, who had always been a joy, began lying in dirt and then rolling on the carpet to scratch her back. Carpet upkeep was wearing me down. I was driven by pride to keep it clean so I wouldn't have to admit that I *might* have picked the wrong carpet for a family with four small children. My carpet cleaner never left my side, and I was getting a touch crabby with the thoughtless children (and dog) who dirtied *my* carpet. Stains not visible in the morning were very noticeable in the late afternoon when I was tired, the house messy and the sun shone through the sliding doors at just the right angle. I was losing the "clean carpet" battle and my perspective.

After two months of this, I surrendered. I admitted to myself that I had made a mistake. I had chosen the wrong carpet. It was not easy to do. I admitted it to my husband and my friends. I gave up trying to keep it spotless and began living with it. I budgeted an amount each month for periodic carpet cleaning. I moved on with my life... until now.

Now, I have "decorated." I have spent many hours wallpapering and painting. After years of living here, the house is finally becoming mine. I am proud of what I did and how nice it all looks—all except for the carpet.

So I've been wondering what I can do about this carpet. If I had the money, what would I put down instead? Again, I've been seeking out advice. But this time from the real experts—other moms.

Some have suggested a wood floor, so we can rollerblade and ride small bicycles on it. Too expensive. "Linoleum," someone quipped, "spills and stains wipe up in a minute." But I have enough trouble mopping my small kitchen floor right now—the whole downstairs might push me over the edge. My closer friends have suggested a concrete block floor with a drain in the middle. Cleanup would involve bringing in the hose and spraying the place down. This is a very attractive idea. One friend went one step better by suggesting we replace the drain with a heavy duty garbage disposal. I liked that. Small toys and leftover food would be no problem for me anymore. She said we would have to warn the children to keep their feet out of the hole and not play with that light switch on the wall... and we'd have to be really careful with the hamster....

So while I'm examining and weighing all of the options, I'm saving for this dream floor as well. I have an envelope in my bill basket marked "floor" that I add to whenever I can. So far I have $42.65. It's been suggested I place a coffee can in my hallway and accept donations or charge visitors when they spill. No matter which fundraising method I use, it will be a while before the wonder floor is installed—plenty of time to carefully plan it all out, again.

# Pillow Fright

## by Deborah Raney

**O**ur eldest daughter Tobi is a strong-willed child. We recognized her independent spirit and her stubborn will almost from the day she was born. While we were living through the challenges of raising a spirited little girl like Tobi, it wasn't always easy to find the humor in things. Fortunately, hindsight has allowed us to see many of those struggles of will in a different light.

One afternoon, when Tobi was at the height of her fiery preadolescent years, she became furious with me because I wouldn't grant her permission to do something. Of course, neither of us can even remember what it was now, but I do recall her anger as she slammed doors and slapped books loudly on the table. I did my best to keep my cool.

"Tobi Anne," I said through clenched teeth, "you are going to ruin something and then we will both be sorry."

My words did little to calm her down, so I took her by the shoulders and escorted her to her room. As we marched down the hall, I had a sudden flashback of myself as a young teen. I had almost forgotten that I'd kicked a door or two myself in those days.

Thinking quickly, I reached for the pillow on Tobi's bed. "You know honey, I remember when I was angry I used to feel like kicking things sometimes, so I understand your need to get your frustrations out. But if you feel like you just have to punch something, beat on something you can't hurt. Here," I told her, "you can punch your pillow to your heart's content." I handed her the pillow and left the room.

All was quiet for quite some time. I was just about to congratulate myself on my brilliant handling of the situation when I heard the muffled sound of fist meeting pillow again and again. Tobi emerged from her room a few minutes later, cool, calm and collected. I smiled smugly to myself and forgot about the whole incident until about a week later.

It was washday and I was methodically stripping all the beds in the house. Removing Tobi's pillowcase, I found myself face-to-face with a larger than life portrait rendered directly on the pillow in colorful marking pens.

Tobi has inherited some of her father's remarkable artistic talent and this portrait was done quite skillfully. In fact, the face on the pillow looked vaguely familiar. Then it struck me: It was as if I was looking into a mirror. It was my face staring back at me from the pillow. As I pictured my daughter methodically drawing my likeness on her pillow and then beating the stuffing out of me with her fists, I laughed so hard I barely could finish the laundry. I was impressed with her creativity—and her will power since she hadn't shown me her handiwork the moment it was completed.

Tobi's portrait punching bag was well used during her remaining years at home. We've told this story many times and Tobi laughs the loudest. Last fall, she went away to college, taking her pillow with her. I'm willing to bet, after hearing the sweetness in her voice over four hundred miles of telephone wire, that now her pillow gets hugged more than hammered.

Three-year-old
Daughter to two psychologists,
Witnesses them arguing,
Screams at each,
"What's your issue?"
Parents, terrified,
Anticipate adolescence.

*Robert Deluty*

# Are We Having Fun Yet?

## by Renee Hawkley

One of the truest equations ever written is "crisis plus time equals humor." Of course, I'm not talking about the hard-core tragedies that involve loss of life or limb. I'm referring to all the "little" accidents and "not-so-little" mishaps that plop themselves down in the middle of a perfectly wonderful day and take possession of your sense of humor until the whole mess is just a memory. Then, as if by magic, the entire traumatic experience turns hilariously funny.

Any mother worth her refrigerator magnets has a few tales to tell. Like the time a five-pound honey container spilled "by accident" in my silverware drawer and went undetected for a couple of hours. I can smile about it now, but I wasn't too cheerful while the honey was still dripping.

Now it's great fun to pull out photos of the kids covered with the chicken pox. I can't remember laughing out loud while applying the Caladryl® and trying to keep them from scratching the scabs.

Then there was the time (one and only) I fed one of my infants an entire jar of strained beets. True, I thought the purple bib and the little purple face were cute. For the next two days, diaper-time wasn't so cute. Now, just the thought of a beet makes me smile.

A friend of mine has a story I've never been able to match. She had continual problems keeping track of

115

her three preschoolers while shopping, so she devised a system. She connected herself to the two older children by tying long lengths of sewing elastic between her wrists and theirs. She imagined that her plan would open a whole new dimension to her shopping, since she would be able to keep track of the two older ones, hold the baby in one arm, and actually have one hand free to "shop." Move over, Edison.

Everything was unfolding beautifully until the family approached the escalator. One child got on. The other couldn't gather the courage and took off screaming in the other direction. Meanwhile, the baby panicked and started to wail. Steven Spielberg should have such an imagination!

I don't imagine you feel much like laughing when you're standing at the bottom of an escalator stretched between two lengths of elastic, listening to one of your children holler "Get on, Mom!" while the other two children are screaming in fear, and all the while disaster is becoming imminent as the elastic pulls tighter and tighter in both directions.

Who knows how the story would have ended if it hadn't been for two concerned bystanders (mothers themselves, most assuredly)? The one at the top of the escalator dashed down the "going up" escalator, picked up the darting child, and loosened the slack in the elastic by continuing to keep one step ahead of the movement of the stairs. In the meantime, the other onlooker picked up the screamer, transported him to the bottom of the escalator, and put him on the moving stairs. At last, mother and her unpredictable brood were reunited at the top of the escalator amidst a flood of tears.

The shopping trip was over. The trip down the escalator and to the car was made without fanfare.... or elastic. A few weeks later, my friend was able to laugh about her story. It's a classic.

Crisis plus time equals humor? Nobody knows the truth of that statement like a mother. That's why nurturing a sense of humor is possibly the best insurance a mother can have that her long-range story will have a happy ending. After all, when you're immersed in a profession of endless surprises, a sense of humor is mandatory. It helps you look back with a smile and ahead with the determination to cope with whatever comes next.

# No One
# Warned Me!

119

# Frogenstein
## by Lisa Suhay

**L**ife is harsh, and as parents we seek to protect our children from sadness where we can. At least, that is what I told myself the morning I sat by the window blow-drying a frog back to life with my hair dryer.

It was one of those balmy spring days that leads to windows being opened for the first time in months. Unfortunately, a large frog managed to get stuck between the window and the screen on our unheated screened-in porch when I cranked the louvered windows shut at night.

The temperature dropped overnight. In the morning my sons, ages two and four, were witness to the frozen creature obstructing their view of the yard. Opening the window allowed the frogsicle to land with a thud on the top of the air conditioner outside. The boys peered out at the still form.

It was awful. The poor thing was lying on its back, arms folded neatly across its chest, knees bent and toes crimped with cold where they had been trapped around the window edge.

"It's dead? What do you mean dead?" demanded Zoltan, age four.

I made a lame attempt at explanation, saying "It was very cold and well…."

"So get it a blanket. Quick, before a bird eats it," he countered.

"Nooooo!" howled Ian, age two. "It brinked its eyes. Fick it, Mom! You fick it, preeeease!"

It did blink. But fick it? Er…um…fix it? Okay. It's frozen, so we should unfreeze it.

Being fresh from the shower and drying my hair, the solution came rather easily to mind.

Sound silly? Am I the only parent who has done things like switched live goldfish for floaters when the kids weren't looking, or told them a movie character was "just sleeping" when it was really the Big Sleep?

When it comes to rough toddler topics, death is even more difficult than where babies come from because it comes up earlier and more often.

It starts with Bambi's mother, then goes on with Simba's father in *The Lion King*. "When we die, our bodies become the grass and the antelope eat the grass," James Earl Jones' rich, fatherly voice intoned shortly before his character became living-impaired. This resulted in my older son sobbing, "Mommy, I don't want to be grass!!!" Thank you, Disney.

So you can see how a mother could be driven to amphibian resurrection. I had dodged the death question bullet for four years, and one more day wasn't going to kill me.

That is how my neighbor, Ray, ended up seeing me at seven o'clock in the morning, blow-drying one of

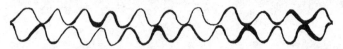

Kermit's cousins through the window screen. It seemed better than the alternative, which was a dip in the bathtub and a few hours spent chasing a revived and frisky frog around the house.

Ray is the father of three girls and was completely unfazed by the sight of Frogenstein coming back to life. Slowly, and I would guess painfully, the frog unfolded. It looked like one of those Chinese paper flowers on the water. It rolled over and shakily hopped off the air conditioner and back into the yard.

"Yeah! Go Mom," Ian shrieked, with a big smile of relief. He hopped over to me. "I give you a frog kiss for dat one, Mom."

My theory is that my children will have to deal with death soon enough. These days of frog kisses are precious, and I can use all that I can get.

# My Son at Twelve

Poised.
Caught between
The world of men,
the world of boys,
He leaves the mall
Smelling of sampled cologne
and
Clutching a bag of jelly beans,
So sweet.

*Linda Wacyk*

# Mean What You Say!

## by Sheila Abood

**O**nce, at a family dinner, I asked my son to pour some more Coke® into my glass. In fact, that is exactly what I said. "Willie, will you pour some more Coke into my glass?"

My nephew Sam looked up and said, as only a sixteen-year-old can, "Gee, Aunt Sheila, where do you think he'd pour it?"

Sam meant to be funny, but in our household one speaks very clearly and never, never assumes anything because my children are very literal-minded. Notice, I didn't say liberal (Independent Baptists don't use such language); I said *literal.*

The first inkling I had of this tendency in my children occurred when Willie was around four. There may have been other instances, but the earliest I remember is when, in a moment of reproof, I told him to watch his mouth.

A moment later, I glanced at him and he was trying to pull his lips out and cross his eyes downward in order to watch his mouth.

Then there was the time I baked a beautifully perfect cherry pie for a church social. I carefully loaded three children into the car and settled the pie on the front seat. It was still warm, so I couldn't use my pie carrier. Remembering that I was responsible for bringing a serving utensil, I opened the door and with eyes

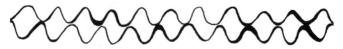

of flint and teeth bared I hissed, "Keep your hands off that pie."

I returned a few seconds later to find three-year-old Amber with her feet in the center of my flaky Crisco® crust. You see, I hadn't told her to keep all her body parts out of the pie—only her hands.

However, all of the above pales beside the following story, which has passed into family legend.

With the birth of our fourth child, we had purchased a station wagon. It was old; in fact, when it was new I had been in the tenth grade, but it was huge, ran well and was cheap. Also, the interior was in excellent condition. I was thrilled. And so I lined up troops, minus the baby, and had a little pep talk.

This was a nice car. We were going to keep it nice. There would be no teeth marks on this padded dash, no tic-tac-toe grids on these vinyl seats, no eating allowed at all, and (I paused for effect) if anyone had to be sick, they would do it on the carpet scraps.

It may seem strange that I felt constrained to include that last bit, but my children throw up the same way some children get nose bleeds. To insure maximum safety, I had inserted large carpet scraps on the floor of the car to protect the incredibly new-looking carpet.

Now fast forward several months. It is July 4th, and in Kearney, Nebraska, the fire department always presents a huge array of fireworks near the high school.

We are there with my mother, parked in the parking lot of the E. V. Free Church. We are seated on the grass and waiting for the sky to darken. It has been a full day with huge helpings of rich homemade ice cream.

Willie suddenly is making his way through the crowd. He weaves over to where I am seated, holding baby Katherine.

"Mom, I feel sick. I..." with that he runs past me. I cannot readily leap up since I have to locate my husband and pass the baby.

When I do reach him, he is standing by the car, vomiting into the backseat.

"What in the Wide World of Sports are you doing?" I ask.

Grandma is there, holding his forehead. When she looks up, the sun glints off her glasses. "He said you said that they had to throw up on the car floor."

"Oh, for heaven's sake! Yes! I said that but I meant if we were hurtling down I-80 at 60 mph. Not if we were out amongst nature in full view of ditches, gutters, trash bins and restrooms!"

We couldn't leave, being hemmed in on all sides by hundreds of cars. I remember a man on a motorcycle with long greasy hair and an earring looking at us like we were barbarians.

The evening ended a trifle downish. Willie continued to feel poorly (it seemed he had consumed three bowls of ice cream mixed with green grapes), I was

lamenting the car's interior, and William felt as though we'd made a spectacle of ourselves.

Six years and a couple of cars have come and gone since then. I've learned to be very circumspect in my speech, but every once in a while I slip up.

Just yesterday I asked Lindsay to put some gas in my car.

# I Am Writing This Because...

### by Rosemary Raymond Horvath

**I** am writing this because I don't want to clean the aquarium. Later this morning I plan to wash the kitchen floor; probably I will sweep the porch instead.

Don't you find that much of mothering is like that? There is so much to do that if you can't get yourself to do one thing, there is always something else waiting in the wings to be done.

For example, I get hives when it's time for science projects. I'd like to meet the genius who thought them up in a dark alley sometime. On science fair weekends while my dear husband coaches three recalcitrant children with their projects, I change all the furniture around. This is called productive escapism.

Ironing is another one of those things. It scares me to death to iron around small children, and since I have been nursing or pregnant for a full third of my life, I can pretty much count on small children hanging around. Therefore, when the laundry room hits terminal mass, I have to do *something.* I clean the garage and mow the lawn.

This is a terrible habit, but it makes me look good. The neighbors don't know that I am painting the gutters because my linen closet is messy. They can't know unless I tell them that I am pruning the trees because

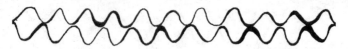

the dishwasher needs to be emptied. If they see me sewing matching dresses for my daughters, they don't realize that otherwise I would have to mend the ones in the basket.

I take the dog for brisk walks because I can't face the bathroom. I organize playgroups for my toddler because my garden needs weeding. I read literature on archaeology because the family room is dirty. (As a matter of fact, it occurs to me that my family room would be a great dig!)

I nurse my babies because bottles look like a lot of trouble. And I do volunteer work because it enables me to talk to adults. (What do we talk about? Children!)

So my house is sort of clean, my kids are pretty well groomed and the dog is exercised—but oh well. The aquarium is still dirty.

# The Eighteen-Month-Old's Guide to Dressing, Dining and Shopping

### by Carol Foster Segal

**W**hen your mother announces that there are no more Cheerios® and that you'll have to go back to the store to buy a new box, lie on your back, kick your feet, cry and scream "Cheerios now." When she carries you to your room to get ready, arch your back, flail your arms and cry some more.

While she's looking for the socks you hid behind the dresser yesterday, climb out of your crib. Open your dresser drawer and put on your knit hat, even though it's August. Say "hat," smile and wrinkle your nose. Your mother will laugh and give you a hug. While she's still looking for socks, pull the hat over your eyes and run around the room. Laugh until you run into something, then cry and ask to be picked up.

Sit quietly on your mother's lap until she has pulled up and cuffed your socks. While she is putting on your right shoe, remove your left sock. Continue in this manner until your mother has dressed the equivalent of four sets of twins.

In the car, try to undo the straps of your safety seat. Whimper off and on. Throw all of your toys on the floor. Three blocks from your destination, settle down

131

and sing "Mom, Mom, Mommy, Mom" to the tune of "Row, Row, Row Your Boat."

In the grocery store, hang over the side of the shopping cart, the harness your mother brought should support you. Try to reach as many cans and jars as possible. Chant the words "cookie," "banana" and "now." Wave to strangers. Pull your mother's hair. Turn around in your seat and unwrap all the rolls of paper towels and toilet paper in the cart. Lift soft, easily bruised items like pears and tomatoes and drop them on the floor. Experiment. Bite into a package of hot dogs, being careful to tear the hermetically sealed plastic wrapper. Do this after your mother has spent fifteen minutes in the checkout line.

When it is time to get back into your car seat, stiffen your body. Do *not* bend your knees. Slide onto the floor two or three times. Give in only when your mother says, "Do you want to have lunch again in your lifetime?" Once you are strapped in and your mother has started the car, sing "do-do-do." Repeat this fifty times. Start to fall asleep, even though this means you will be cranky when you arrive home.

At home, do not sit quietly with your toys. Instead, help your mother unpack the groceries. Place the four-pound bag of cat food on the cat. Remove all grapes from their stems. While your mother is apologizing to the cat and picking up the grapes, take a package of frozen mixed vegetables (it should be slightly soggy), carry it into the living room and place it in the middle of the couch.

When you see your mother unpack a box of Cheerios, you can a) resume your earlier position on the kitchen floor and throw another tantrum or b) attempt to scale your highchair. Option B is preferable; your mother probably will help you. She may even let you have Cheerios for lunch.

When seated, line up your bowl of cereal and your cup of milk. Take the dry Cheerios and drop them into your milk. Look up at your mother and grin. She will say, "It's a good thing you're cute." When your Cheerios are no longer floating, remove them one by one. It is important to use the back of your spoon, so that the Cheerios fall onto your tray before you can eat them. Then pick up a fistful and cram it into your mouth. Milk will dribble down your chin, into your collar, up your arms into the sleeves of your t-shirt and past the pocket of your bib onto your overalls.

Repeat this step until all of the Cheerios have disappeared. Then hold out your bowl and say "more." If your mother refills your bowl, stick out your lower lip and refuse to eat. If your mother offers you a banana instead, pretend it is a telephone. Say "hi, hi," then mash it into your ear and hair. Your mother will announce, "Lunch is over. It's time for your nap. I need a rest."

# School Days

School days are here to stay.
Mothers now have time to play!
Lunch to pack and snacks to bake;
Costumes for the play to make.
Books to cover, forms to fill;
The teacher asks for help: Who will?
Meetings day and meetings night;
The children's bedroom is a sight!
Volunteer at all the schools
is among the golden rules.
Help with homework is a must;
Who has time to sweep or dust?
Read a story—no TV!
All the sports events to see.
Music lessons, scouting too;
Someone always has the flu!
Clothes to wash, food to buy;
The price of gas has gone sky high!
Yes, school days are here to stay.
Mothers have NO time to play!

*Julie A. Nelson*

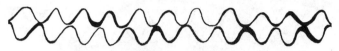

# Do You Hear What I Hear?

### by Donna Marcinkowski DeSoto

**M**y soon-to-be four-year-old daughter wakes up every morning with the same question: "What day is it today?" If I don't answer, "Saturday" or "Sunday," she sighs and then mutters, "Darn it. Is he already gone?"

Thus begins the countdown for the hour that never, ever comes soon enough, when we get to go and wait in the carpool line for her beloved eight-and-one-half-year-old brother Andy.

"Will Andy be home for lunch today?"

"No, not today. That's only on Mondays."

"Darn it. Do we get to go to Andy's class to help the kids write today?"

"No, that's on Fridays."

"Darn. Then what do we get to do today?"

"First you have ballet with your friends, and then we get to go to our office for a while."

Her response is a lukewarm, "Is that it?"

Try as I do to busy her with this precious one-on-one time together—we paint and color, play beauty shop, take field trips to skating rinks and bowling alleys, go for long walks looking for bugs and "rattle-snakes," wash fingerprints off windows and walls, most of this with heavy doses of giggling and girl talk—none

of this entices her the way Andy's world does. She is fascinated by his intricate construction-toy creations. The music that flows from the keyboard he plays gives her uncontrollable "happy feet." He is a wonderful vet to all of her sick stuffed animals. And the covers of the Hardy Boys books he reads are "so awesome" that she keeps a stack of them hidden under her bed. She is also determined that she will find a way to go to the bathroom standing up! I wonder if I should have sent her to preschool this year.

"I know. Let's make muffcakes today for Andy and for Daddy." The last time we made these, she personalized them: miniature marshmallows and pretzel pieces covered the top of Andy's, and she delightedly plopped green olives on top of her daddy's, "because he loves them so much."

Later, "You know, Mommy, I want to be a room mother when I grow up," she happily announced, at 2:50 p.m. from her car seat behind me. I am proud and flattered.

The sun of her universe (and the son of mine) finally appears from the jumble of 600 kids squeezing through two doors. But all is not well, because it is about to happen again. I count to ten, take several deep breaths, and whisper a quick prayer. Help me be patient. Help me stay calm. Don't let it happen today, but if it does, and I know it will, help us to get home safely.

"Hi!" We all holler in unison, as the car door swings open.

I lean over to hug my second-grader, who appears to have gotten bigger during this seven-hour absence from me. "How was your day?"

Andy: "Pretty good."

Aimee: "Pretty good."

Uh-oh.

Andy: "Mommy, she's starting again."

Me: "Aimee, you've been waiting all day for Andy to come home. Why don't you tell him what we did today? Remember the tent we made in the dining room?"

Andy: "See, she won't say anything until I do."

Aimee: "See, she won't say anything until I do."

Andy: "Mom-my! "

Aimee: "Mom-my! "

Me: "Andy, just try to ignore her when she starts copying you and she'll stop."

Andy: "But I can't ignore it."

Aimee: "But I can't ignore it."

Andy: "Aimee, please. You're a real pain."

Aimee: "Aimee, please. You're a real pain."

Several silent minutes pass. We are almost home, but I still don't have a good feeling about this.

Andy: "Thank goodness. Now I can get a little peace and R and R."

Aimee: "Thank goodness. Now I can get a little peace and—what did he say?"

Me: "R and R. That means rest and relaxation."

Aimee: "What is relaxation?"

Me: "It is like a nice rest. What I'll need if we ever get home."

Aimee: "Oh. But Andy, will you still play with me when we get home?"

Andy: "I guess so."

I breathe a quiet, incredulous sigh of relief.

Aimee: "Great. I love you."

Remember how the pain of childbirth magically seems to vanish when you first cradle that new baby in your arms? So it is that I survive these inevitable episodes of sibling rivalry; I cherish the perhaps too few and far between moments of genuine brotherly and sisterly love.

As I pull into the driveway, Aimee is doing that familiar car seat lean, complete with very un-dainty snores. Time now to steal some one-on-one with my firstborn. "Come on in, Andy. Let's go have a snack."

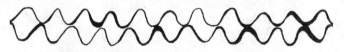

# Reflections in the Checkout Line

### by Sheila Abood

**T**he line was endless—winding through aisles three, four and five. I could see the cashier and customers in the distance; they looked about twelve inches high. It was going to be the mother of all waits, and it would be at least twenty minutes before I got close enough to the tabloid display to read about the woman who gave birth to a baby gorilla.

My seventeen-year-old daughter, Amber, and I had been shopping, but I was beginning to wonder if the merchandise in my cart was important enough to go through menopause in a checkout line. It had already been a memorable day I would have liked to forget, and as the cart behind me scraped my Achilles heel for the third time, I slowly pivoted with an icy glare only to meet the openly envious gaze of the woman behind me.

Our eyes locked and after a full five seconds, she gushed, "Oh, I wish I was like you. I can't wait until my kids are as old as your daughter." If her son hadn't jammed the sharp-edged frame of his mother's cart into my shins, I might have told her the truth. Instead, I merely smiled smugly and stood to the side of my cart.

The line advanced somewhat, the checker and cash register were slowly attaining near-normal dimensions, and I could step back and analyze her reaction.

Her cart was filled with what amounted to a small fortune in disposable diapers and the paraphernalia of childhood. My cart held three bottles of shampoo, two of conditioner, two bottles of French lilac body spray, a large bottle of nail polish remover, one bottle of Hush-Hush pink nail polish, one bottle of Ripe Mango nail polish, a twelve-pack of panty hose and one bottle of dog shampoo.

Her seven-year-old was wiping his nose on the sock display, and my daughter was silently examining her nails. I had to admit it—the mother of the young nosewiper behind me definitely appeared to have gotten the fuzzy side of the lollipop.

I could have told her the truth and sent her naive expectations directly into the dumpster, but I didn't. She wouldn't have believed me anyway. Ten years ago, I wouldn't have. I wouldn't have wanted to. But the pure, unalterable truth is that it doesn't get any easier, the kids just get bigger.

For example, Amber and I appeared to be standing companionably side-by-side, with nary a discouraging word between us. Actually, we weren't speaking to each other. That's because in aisle 13 Amber asked if she could go to Trish's party. Trish, who is more of a friend of a friend of a friend, was having a party to celebrate her parents being in Alaska. "Sorry," (I really wasn't), "but the house rule is no parents, no can go."

"But, Mom," she wailed, "her brother will be there!"

"Oh, I feel much better," I said. "Why don't you borrow my prayer leader's guide and you can have a

140

Bible study there. Her nineteen-year-old brother can bring over his friends."

As for the contents of my cart, none of it was for me. Well, that's not entirely true. I'm sure that Bridgit, our dog, would share her shampoo with me if I really needed it.

At one time, I too had my innocent dreams. I can remember thinking that someday things would get easier—that I would be able to rush into a darkened bathroom without first checking to see if a poopy diaper was there. Now I never get to rush into any bathroom; I have to fidget at the locked door and by turns plead, cajole, threaten and bribe to gain entry. Having gained entry, I am forced to carry on the most personal of duties while ducking the electrical cord of a daughter's curling iron as she pats and preens.

There was a time when I really looked forward to a bathroom free of toys. I yearned to take a shower without Barbie® leering at me from behind the shampoo. I just knew she was laughing at me!

But while there are fewer Barbies and baby dolls to be found, like so many beached whales, they are being replaced with skin-cleansing pads, disposable razors, and spongy eye shadow applicators .

After the birth of each of my children, I also recollect reading a lot of cute little articles—"Is There Sex After Birth?" or "How to Manage Your Intimate Life with Your Newborn."

Heck, having a love life with little kids was easy. I mean, the kids went to sleep at nine or ten, and while

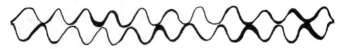

they may have awakened in the middle of the night and cried, at least they weren't pounding on the bedroom door asking for the next day's lunch money. Teenagers are like hamsters. They are awake all night, running up and down the halls looking for towels and taking showers and arguing about who's next to use the hair dryer.

The teenage birth rate would decline dramatically if they were forty-something and married with teenagers...a complicated idea I'll admit but one worthy of investigation.

Mostly I guess I expected that my children, upon looking like adults, would act as adults. I didn't realize that while the outsides were racing pell-mell towards maturity, the insides were proceeding at a much slower rate. In fact, the only difference between a preschooler and an adolescent is size, hormones and a driver's license.

Take a tired, cranky two-year-old to the mall and after witnessing his temper tantrums, some little blue-haired matron will come up, pat you on the arm and whisper conspiratorially, "Someone needs a nap." Twelve years later, take that same cranky, tired kid to the mall and someone is likely to thrust a pamphlet for a drug rehab center into your hands.

Ten years ago, I was thirty-one and the mother of four. Ten years and one child later, life has only gotten more complicated.

It's a tricky business, this raising older kids. They need me a lot more now (let's face it—toddlers don't

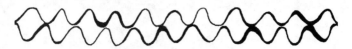

get caught up in drugs and sex) but it's a lot more hands-off maintenance. They need my ears and my heart a lot more than my advice and opinions. And they need me to consistently take a stand.

Last week, Amber was bemoaning the fact that I wouldn't allow her to see a certain show. "Ooooh, isn't she so stupid?" she inquired of my twenty-year-old son. "Nobody is as stupid as she is."

At that point, my son Willie—my first born—the one who can never remember the trash needs empty-ing, redeemed himself for all the wrenches he has ever run through the washer and dryer. He said, "That just shows that she's got high morals, and I'm glad I was raised that way."

Amber rushed to be sick in the trash basket and I decided I needed to make a batch of Willie's favorite cinnamon rolls.

Now, I didn't relate that story just to impress you (well maybe just a teensy bit), but I've learned that what I'm doing makes a difference. Staying home with my older children is valid, rewarding and necessary. Despite the fact that this job has no insurance, profit sharing or retirement plans, I think it's the most impor-tant job in the world.

# Priorities

When they were babies
it was a constant chore
to keep the debris
from off the floor.

They'd crawl and they'd scoot
under table and chair,
and eat any stuff
that they found down there.

So I constantly swept
and picked up the clutter,
and occasionally then
you'd hear me mutter:

"Will I always be rushing
with scrub rag and broom?
Will I never have time
for cleaning this room?"

Well, years do fly fast—
now those same boys are tall,
their handprints have moved
further up on the walls.

And now there is time
for me to clean floors,
but—the funny thing is—
it doesn't matter anymore.

'Cause they no longer crawl,
or drop food down the grates,
they dine at the table—
with manners! and plates!

And I no longer fret
about more time to clean,
now I'm too busy cooking
for these hungry teens!

*Gayle Urban*

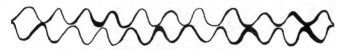

# The Shower

## by Robin Patterson

One of the greater pleasures of my life is climbing into a nice hot shower. The drumming beat and the rising steam block out all other sights and sounds, creating a cozy cocoon where soothing hot water pummels away at the tension between my shoulder blades. It's the perfect escape. Almost.

My shower door is clear glass; there are three reasons for this. The first reason (and I am sure many clear doors are sold because of this) is so that I will be able to see Anthony Perkins if he comes after me with a knife. If you don't know what I'm talking about, *never* watch the movie *Psycho*. This will keep your showers free of irrational paranoia. The second reason is that opaque shower doors make me claustrophobic, which doesn't help my irrational paranoia. The third—and most important—reason is so that I can see what my kids are up to. My children are never up to much in the bathroom; the boys generally do their best to avoid water that doesn't come from a hose, squirt gun or balloon. When *I* hit the showers, however, it is another story. They are drawn to the bathroom like puppies to a slipper. Trouble invariably follows.

I don't understand why hostilities escalate when I'm in the shower. I always try to leave Mr. Rogers in charge! Nevertheless, I am called upon to break up fights and disagreements from my steamy sanctuary, and I can tell you that being dripping wet really under-

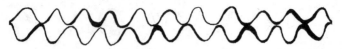

mines a parent's authority. I am often called upon to pass judgment on all sorts of disputes between my sons. The customary complaints include such classics as: "Mom, I had the couch first!" "Mom, he's chewing with his mouth open!" and of course, "Mom, he's looking at me!"

Inevitably, while I'm dispensing justice with the wisdom of a sopping wet Solomon, my youngest son creeps, unnoticed, into the bathroom. I return to my soapy reverie for a minute or so before I realize that he is peacefully sitting there watching me—and sucking on the toothpaste tube. (Have you ever wiped your hands on a towel that turns out to be covered with toothpaste? This only begins to plumb the depths of my dislike of toothpaste—but that's another story.)

"See my boaties, Mommy?" he says sweetly. I cast my eyes upon the harbor in my sink. I suppose I always knew my mascara would float, but I was surprised to find my eye shadow and blush cruising right alongside! Bubbles on the surface alerted me that something was submerged. Ah, a roll of toilet paper had met the same fate as the Titanic.

Occasionally I am tempted to preserve the peace of my shower by locking the door, but of course that would be unkind. Anyway, my kids can pick the lock.

# Games
# We
# Play

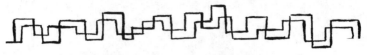

# Life's a Ball

### by Cheryl-Ann Hughes

**I**t's late at night, our four children are in bed and my husband comes toward me slowly. "Okay," he whispers in a voice husky with urgency, "We're on the same team; I've got the ball." He demonstrates how he wants me to stand. "If you plant your feet between me and the man guarding me, your guy will leave you to guard me. You roll left unprotected, I pass it to you. You take a shot and bingo, we score!"

It's called a "pick and roll" and although every basketball player in the country, including my ten-year-old daughter, can demonstrate it flawlessly, I just don't get it. So my husband patiently tries, once again, to explain this move in one of our late night lessons, during which I try to learn more about the game that has become such a large part of my family life.

When I married this basketball nut sixteen years ago, I assumed that his passionate love of the game would affect me only marginally. At the time, "pick and roll" sounded like something you did with your hair and basketball was only a hobby.

That was before my children became infatuated with the game and before I realized that my life and basketball are forever and inextricably linked. Even after our children were born, I labored under the delusion that I could guide them toward other pastimes. Our daughter, I figured, would be mine to mold. She could take up dancing or maybe figure skating. Like-

wise, I assumed that under my direction, my sons could become—and I know this is a stretch—but I thought that maybe, just maybe, they could become men who enjoyed things like the theater or a really good historical novel. Looking back, it seems incredibly naïve, but I did try—museums, libraries, the Kennedy Center. You name it, if it seemed even remotely child-friendly and had some historical or cultural value, we did it.

Sometimes my husband even came along, although I now realize that he was merely keeping a low profile until they all got old enough to dribble a ball. That didn't take long at all and dribbling quickly led to passing, blocking and shooting. Basketball became not merely a weekend activity but something they did every night. At first it was cute and I was indulgent.

After dinner, "the guys" would go outside to shoot some hoops. Dad was usually the shooter and the boys just ran around trying to block him. Okay, I thought, let him have his fun, I can wait. But the boys didn't seem to tire of it. After a while, even my daughter joined in, quickly becoming one of them. Soon, our dinner conversations became preludes to the after dinner shoot-arounds, as plays were discussed and teams reshuffled at the table.

Then there were the basketball videos. I'd find my whole family cuddled on the couch watching some expert demonstrate the perfect "give and go" or the exact way to extend your arm to make a three-point shot. All of this information was digested a lot more readily than any of the historical facts I'd been cramming down their throats since they were old enough to listen.

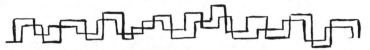

There were outside influences as well. The neighborhood kids were in league with my husband from the beginning. I learned that basketball can be fun when played with two or ten. It can be played in the street, in the pool, in the schoolyard. I even have found children, and sometimes adults, bouncing a basketball off my family room wall. Slowly, almost without realizing it, my children began to love the game as much as their father does.

It wasn't until I watched my oldest son play in his first organized game that I knew the battle was over. He glowed with excitement; basketball sparks a fire in him like nothing I have ever seen before. Since that time, my second son has also started to play organized basketball with such joy that I smile just thinking about him on the court. Also, this year, my husband coached our daughter's fourth grade team while our youngest waited impatiently on the sidelines for time-outs so that he could go out on the court and shoot his ball.

We don't get to many museums these days. We do, however, spend a lot of time together watching, analyzing and learning the game of basketball. I've come to realize that although I certainly have a strong impact on who my children are, my passions will never be theirs. I've found that if I want to be a part of their lives, I am going to have to learn to play ball.

So the lessons continue. Sometimes I learn about basketball and sometimes I learn about life. But then, in our house, they're one and the same.

## One-Year-Old
## with Potato Chip

Competing pleasures,
Tactile and gustatory.
Shall I crush or eat

*Robert Deluty*

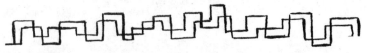

# The Mom Olympics

### by Carole Wright

"**T**hanks for joining us, folks, for today's segment of Mom Olympics. Jim and I will be providing the play-by-play action. Today we have one of the most challenging events, the Park Walk."

"This event, Bob, though it may not seem so on the surface, is comparable to a triathlon. The participant must be able to perform strongly in many areas: speed, agility, stamina and endurance."

"How does the scoring work, Jim?"

"Good question, Bob. These events are scored for length of time, and the amount of activities included in that time span. There is no time limit; it's up to the athlete to know when to wind down the event so she doesn't completely collapse before she gets home."

"What about training, Jim?"

"The training varies with each participant, Bob. The more years of experience they have, the better they do with preparation, handling emergencies and overall knowledge of the game. On the other hand, the longer they've been in training the more likely they are to be physically spent, susceptible to injuries such as strains, or just mentally fatigued."

"Well, thanks for the background! Let's go down to the neighborhood where the event is about to begin. Who's our first contestant today, Jim?"

"We've got a thirty-four-year-old mother, Bob. Prior to becoming a professional mom, she was competent in many sporting activities. This certainly helps; any kind of physical training is always an asset. Nevertheless, as we've heard many entrants testify, 'No matter what kind of training you've had, nothing prepares you for Motherhood.'"

"She looks like she's in fairly good physical shape, too."

"Yes, I agree. She has put on some extra weight with each child, but that's pretty typical. One other factor here, she has a one-year-old, which means no sleep for the past year. I do see some bags under her eyes, but she's also got a look of determination in them."

"Great. Now let's see... this mother has four years' experience?"

"Right. She's got a four-year-old in addition to the baby. She's bringing along her son's friend, who is also four. That adds an element of difficulty to the routine, and she'll get extra points for that.

"And there she goes, out the door. The one-year-old daughter will be pushed in the stroller. The son will be riding his bike, which is a standard two-wheeler. The friend will be on the son's old bike, also a two-wheeler, but with training wheels."

"Yes, I see the friend is not too sure of himself—a little off-balance. This could add an interesting degree of difficulty."

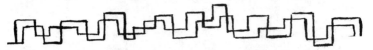

"They're only about three blocks from the park, although they do have one major street to cross, and they'll get the standard points for that."

"And I see they've made it across safely. Nice, smooth transition there—you can see that she's done this walk hundreds of times."

"Exactly, Bob, yet I love to watch this event because it's the unexpected things that really give the opportunity to see the skill and handling techniques of these mothers. This is where the real professionalism of the sport comes in, Bob. There has to be a balance. What equipment is essential? What can be left behind? Bringing too much along can really slow you down, especially when stuff starts falling out of the top of the stroller. Not having the one essential item you need, for instance an extra diaper, could in some cases cause the whole trip to be aborted."

"Fascinating, Jim. Well, I see they've entered the park."

"Yes, they're cutting across diagonally and the first area they come to is the bike trail. The terrain's pretty rough here. Pushing a stroller across this stuff wreaks havoc on the back muscles. There's a series of little hills and then one large hill where the trail begins. They're approaching that now and they need to get over it to get to the pond area. The son's pedaling hard and he's going to fly right up. A little trouble here with the friend. He's only about one-third of the way up and he's not going to make it."

"Will she help him?"

"No, she tells him to get off and push it up himself. The judges will deduct two-tenths of a point for that, but I think it was a wise decision. At this point she really needs to conserve her strength. Now they've all reached the crest of the hill and I see a problem arising very quickly. The friend doesn't know how to brake his bike. This is something she should have checked out on flat terrain. This oversight could really cost her, Bob. He's picking up speed and appears to be heading straight for the pond. Of course this is where the years of experience will come into play. Does she run? Does she wait? If she decides to go for it she'll have to throw the brakes on the stroller and run like mad to get him. The key is all in the line of the bike. Will it hit the water at its present course? Her angle judgment at this point is crucial."

"And she's right on the money, Jim. The kid just barely misses the pond and is veering off to the left."

"Yes, she's made the right decision. Her years of mothering experience really show, Bob."

"I agree. Also, it's obvious that her extensive training by taking so many walks here has paid off. She was able to figure in the slope of the hill, the angle, the bike speed, the weight of the child—she did a great job and the energy she saved will help her later."

"Okay. Now they're on the sidewalk that circles the pond. They're still on a slightly downhill angle and I see her son's baseball cap has blown off and gotten stuck in the chain of his bike. You know, Bob, that's

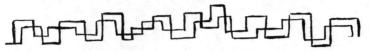

why I love this sport; there's always the unexpected element."

"She's working on the hat now and maybe you can see—it's really jammed in there."

"If she just yanks it out with all her might then you've got the possibility of pulling the chain off and that would be a major problem."

"Okay, now I noticed when she stopped the stroller to work on the bike, she put the stroller brakes on."

"Yes, and she'll get the mandatory two points for that. But wait—this is classic. We have another variable here. The brother has taken the brakes off and is pushing the stroller forward—it's heading straight for the pond! She sees it... no question on this one, Bob, she's running for all she's worth—and she's got it! Great save! Big expenditure of energy for that one. I don't think the judges will deduct any points regarding the brakes. She did have them on—it's just one of those unforeseens."

"Yeah, she did a great job, Jim, but this will definitely tire her out."

"It's back to a steady pace now. She was able to get the hat out of the chain and I believe they're heading back. Just a few side notes to mention here as she's walking. A lot of these things we don't notice initially, but they're crucial to the success of the walk. It's amazing to see the planning and strategy that are involved before the event even starts. She put sunscreen on all the kids; they all want drinks and she's gotten that

taken care of. I see she has tissues for the runny noses and the little one is eating the crackers she brought."

"Amazing preparation, Jim. Well, they've crossed the major street and are heading back. I see some potential trouble here; the friend is tipping over sideways every time he comes to the areas where the driveways slope into the street."

"Yeah, he's fallen about three times now. Every time he tips, she has to try to grab him, while at the same time pushing the stroller. If they can just make it around the corner, they'll be off the major street and he can ride where it's level."

"Oh no! There he goes again, and this time he went all the way over. He's fine, but the training wheel has broken completely off."

"Okay. She's got to push the stroller with one hand now and balance him on the bike with the other. The trick is to keep the bike perfectly level. If it tips even two inches to the wrong side, then the broken training wheel is going to scrape and stop the bike."

"Yes, you can see she's walking in an extremely uncomfortable position."

"I'm sure at this point she's on the edge of utter exhaustion. The kids are hot—the baby's starting to fuss. This is where you have to put out every ounce of effort you've got."

"She's doing great, Jim, and I see she's going to try to get a drink for herself."

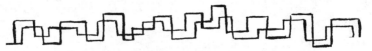

"This will be her last opportunity to score a few points. If she can take a drink and not stop, she can gain some extra points. She's going to give the stroller a push, grab the water and try to get a drink. She's only got about two to three steps to do this and it's not quite enough time, so she'll use the 'stomach thrust,' where she'll let the bar of the stroller jam into her stomach and then shove forward to keep it going. That allows her the few extra steps she needs for a drink."

"Great! She did it smoothly. Now I notice she's not putting the water bottle back, Jim. What's the reason for that?"

"I think she's going to try to hang on to it, Bob, rather than get off balance. She's only about three houses away from home. Her hand is sweaty and the bottle is slipping. She has it by the neck, between her middle and fourth finger while she's pushing the stroller with her thumb and index finger. The real test will be to see if she can get them all up the curb incline in that position. It's nearly an impossible task—but she does it!"

"Fascinating walk, Jim. We'll have the scores here in a minute. You can see she's on the verge of collapse. The kids seem to have their second wind now and are all bouncing around with tons of energy! And here's the score—9.9! Fantastic! What does she get, Jim?"

"She gets to do it all over again tomorrow."

# Katie

Our five-year-olds were happily playing cards
Katie can read, exulted her mother.
Katie, come here,
Katie, come here!
Katie, read this headline.
Katie complied, perfectly yet joylessly,
Then quickly returned to my daughter
And resumed smiling.

Katie's really special, I remarked later.
She sure is, beamed my daughter.
She can shuffle!

*Robert Deluty*

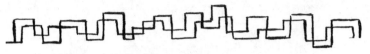

# The Lesson that Wouldn't End

### by Laura M. Jones

**L**et me admit up front that I know it was all my fault. I wouldn't have ended up in the situation if I had been paying attention and following the rules.

It began the day I went to visit a good friend who lived about thirty minutes away. I always loved to go to her home: my three-year-old son, Nate, would play happily with her two children who were close in age, and my five-month-old daughter, Rachel, was content to observe all the activity. So I lingered too long over my last cup of tea, and got everyone organized and into the car much later than I should have. My friend quickly drew a map of a shortcut to the highway that might save me some time, and we said good-bye.

As I juggled her map on my lap, I tried to follow my three-year-old's flow of chatter and make a mental list of all the things I needed to do before we left for vacation the next morning. We were going to stay in a small cabin in a state park in West Virginia, so I was supposed to have already bought groceries to take along. I should have done the laundry and organized some toys and supplies. As I worried, I twisted the map, trying to get oriented.

That's when the flashing lights on the car behind me got my attention.

163

"Mommy! Why did you stop? Is that a police car?"

I explained that I had probably been speeding. I did have a vague memory of zooming along a little fast as my thoughts had zoomed around my head.

"Mommy! What is the policeman's name? Why were you speeding? What is speeding? Is he going to take you to jail?"

Why did Nate sound so pleased at that prospect? "No, he won't take me to jail. Please be quiet while I talk to the policeman."

He duly arrived at my car window, took a look at my wide-eyed son, sleeping baby, scrawled map and driver's license, and went back to his patrol car to write out my ticket.

"Mommy! What is a ticket? How much will you have to pay? Can I be the one to tell Daddy?"

I agreed he could tell Daddy. I was glad he was looking forward to it, since I certainly wasn't. My husband is not a big fan of wasted money.

The rest of the drive home was uneventful. Daddy was fully informed of the incident, I promised everyone that I would be more attentive to speed limits, and I paid my debt to society. I considered the lesson learned and the event forgotten. We had a pleasant vacation, despite my poor preparation.

After we returned, the children and I made one of our frequent trips to the grocery store. Nate immediately trotted down to the end of the first aisle and waited for me to catch up. This was unusual, but I

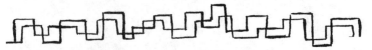

didn't worry. He was just standing there, waiting. As we approached, he leapt into the center of the aisle, palm upraised in the classic stance.

"STOP! You are going too fast! I'm going to have to give you a ticket!" he announced in the powerful voice he had inherited from his father. He whipped out an imaginary pad and pencil and started to write up my imaginary ticket.

The incident had obviously only been forgotten by me. I looked around at the other adults in the aisle. Was that woman contemplating one-percent versus two-percent milk snickering over there? The man picking out a carton of eggs was openly grinning at me. I smiled sheepishly back, paid Nate in imaginary money, and zipped around the corner to the next lane.

"Nate, wouldn't you like to help me pick out some crackers? You can choose what kind we'll buy."

He wasn't about to be distracted. He again trotted down to the end of the aisle and waited. As I approached him, I suggested he might like to help load the cat food into the cart, but he didn't hesitate.

"STOP! You are going too fast!" The scenario was starting again. I proclaimed that I had already *paid* my ticket, I *wasn't* going too fast, and did he want to choose the *ice cream?*

Even the prospect of ice cream wasn't equal to the pleasure of his new game. I had to pay my second imaginary ticket and Nate ran around to wait at the end of aisle three.

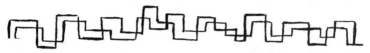

We went through the game again. An elderly man picking out peanut butter looked over and laughed. "Had a little run-in with the law, did you?" I pleaded that I hadn't really been going all that fast, it was my one and only speeding ticket, that I was usually a very careful driver, especially when I had my precious children in the car.

By aisle seven I wasn't feeling all that appreciative of my precious son, however. I was feeling totally out of imaginary money, but Nate had an endless supply of imaginary tickets. We finally reached the checkout counter.

"My mom got a ticket from a *policeman!*" Nate announced. "She was *speeding!*" Not for the first time I regretted my son's eagerness to talk to strangers.

"Oh, really!" the clerk looked at me with raised eyebrows. "How fast was she going?"

Luckily Nate didn't know. "It wasn't that fast," I hurriedly explained. "I don't normally get tickets."

"Uh huh," the clerk answered dubiously. Nate was clearly very familiar with the process and told her all about it.

The policeman-in-the-aisle-of-the-grocery-store game went on for weeks. It was the lesson that wouldn't end. Nate learned to read the car's speedometer and would keep me informed as to my speed. He started to sound quite professional, and I began to fantasize about his future career in law-enforcement. He seemed a natural, with his law-abiding temperament and delight in

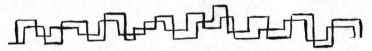

handing out tickets. I wondered if that policeman had any idea that day just how many times I would have to replay my transgression.

But like I said, I know it was all my fault.

Graduation day—
Under their robes,
T-shirts and tattoos.

*Robert Deluty*

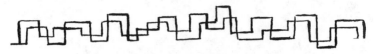

# Just Don't Act
# Like a Mother

### by Renee Hawkley

**R**ecently, my teenage boys paid me the ultimate compliment of allowing me to go shopping with them. Of course, there were a couple of conditions. Number one. I had to bring my purse. The one with the checkbook. Number two. As they put it, "If you come, you can't act like a mother."

"What do you mean by that?" I asked.

"You know. Don't touch us," one of them offered.

"Yeah," piped in the second, "and don't talk like you love us or tell us to stand up straight."

"Just don't look at us," the third added.

"Okay," I said. "Let me get this straight. I can come if I don't touch you, talk to you or look at you."

"That's pretty much it," they agreed.

Well. Who could turn down an offer like that?

So, off we went to the mall in search of P.E. sweats and a couple of pairs of shoes.

If I may take the opportunity to boast, I behaved myself to perfection. Eyes straight ahead. Mouth shut. Hands to myself. The perfect example of apathy. There may have been a few educated mall-goers who guessed that I was the mother of these "dudes" by virtue of

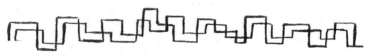

having teenagers of their own. But they certainly didn't get any hints from me.

Well, we bought what we came for and then split up to do some independent browsing. The boys went to Pederson's, a sporting goods store, and I headed for a sale at "Just Petites," my favorite clothing shop.

"What does 'petite' mean?" the youngest one asked one of his brothers before we separated.

"Short," says one of his older brothers. "It's a shop for short girls."

"Why don't they call it 'Just Short'?" asked the first.

I shook my head, rolled my eyes and agreed to meet them at Pederson's in thirty minutes. Twenty minutes later, they were back.

"Mom, what's taking so long? We want to show you something," said one.

"Mom, come on. Somebody might see us in here," said another.

"Alright, alright. I'm coming," I said.

In Pederson's, they directed me to the object of their affection, a hot pink snowboard. They looked me straight in the eye and asked, "Isn't it great, Mom? Don't you just love it?"

"You're looking at me," I said. "People might get ideas."

"Come off it, Mother," another one said as he grabbed my arm and pulled me in the direction of the skateboards. "You've got to see this 'rad' board."

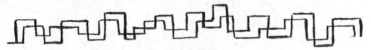

"You're touching me," I reminded him. "What if someone thinks we're related?"

"Mom, get real. This is important."

The other boy called me from the ski department, loud enough for everyone in the store to hear. "Mom, aren't these skis the best? Wouldn't they be great for Christmas?"

"Not so loud," I said as I sauntered over to the ski department, "and don't call me Mom in public. It's embarrassing."

On the way to the car, I asked them if I passed the test well enough to be invited to go shopping again.

"Sure, Mom," they agreed. "Except you acted a little strange in Pederson's."

"What are you smiling for?" one of them asked.

"You didn't tell me I couldn't smile," said I.

## Watering Geraniums

Lifting leaves to water potted geraniums
wintering on a low, sunny windowsill,
I pause
noting the small plastic dinosaurs
in the prehistoric jungle of my young son's imagination.

*Elizabeth Ahmann*

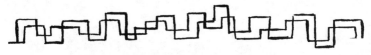

# Herd Ball Mom
### by Kim Burns

**M**y five-year-old son plays herd ball. The league organizers call it micro-soccer. But I've seen soccer, and this is not soccer. A bunch of little boys run *en masse* up and down the field, pausing to kick madly at each other's shins until the ball is popped, completely by chance, out of the scrum. The herd then runs off, sometimes in the direction of the ball.

On my son's team there are two boys who can actually play soccer. They are the coach's sons. But lack of skill isn't hurting the team; it's the lack of concentration that is killing them. Of the five players on the team, only one or two are playing soccer at any given time. The others are too busy.

William is the team entertainer. Each Saturday he cracks up the rest of the team with the old "orange rind in front of your teeth" smile and the always hilarious dizzy drunk walk. I suspect William's parents throw a lot of cocktail parties.

Nathaniel is the nature lover. He supplements the action on the field with bird watching and insect collecting. Nat thoughtfully calls over his teammates to see every interesting specimen. This drives the coach crazy when it happens during a game.

Charles joined the soccer team because he gets to drink from a water bottle. After each run down the field, Charles stumbles over to his mother on the side-

lines and, with award-winning drama, croaks, "Water." Charles spends the last quarter of the game clutching himself and doing a little two-step dance.

Robert is confused about *fútbol* and football. He dazzles the crowd with fancy footwork. He runs down the field, head fakes to the left, cuts right, does the Heisman Trophy pose, then slides into home. Maybe next year he'll incorporate the ball into these moves.

Nicholas may be the reincarnation of a gold miner. The kid cannot pass a patch of bare ground without digging in it. The field we play on has a bare spot at midfield. It calls to Nicholas. During the first play of the game he will shuffle his feet to kick up some dust. The next trip downfield, he might give the dirt a few toe kicks. Two minutes into the game, he is sitting in the middle of the field happily digging, unaware of any action around him.

Nicholas, William, Robert, Charles, Anthony, Nathaniel—together they sound like the roster for a law firm rather than a kids' soccer team. About half of the team members have these formal names. The other half are named Matthew. You would think that having several players with the same name would cause confusion during the game. But our coach ingeniously uses this as a strategy. He will yell, "Matthew, kick the ball," or "Matthew, run downfield!" This catches the attention of several players and sometimes one will actually follow directions. The coach's other strategy is to yell, "This way, this way," and point to the correct goal.

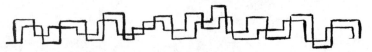

A team of twelve little boys requires an enormous staff of adults. In addition to the coach, we have an assistant coach, ten shoe-tiers, dozens of cheerleaders and a coach's wife. You can always spot the coach's wife in a crowd. She's the one with a line deepening between her eyes and the large folder of papers. The coach's wife is in charge of the game schedule, the practice schedule, the snack schedule, the fundraising schedule and the party schedule.

The coach's wife also planned the end-of-season banquet. It was a lavish affair hosted by a local pizza joint. William provided the afternoon's entertainment by stuffing an entire pizza slice into his mouth at once. The boys laughed until soda came out of their noses. And everyone received a nice plaque with an engraving of a herd ball.

# Toddlersaurus

Lurching, lumbering, careening flat-footed,
Oblivious to obstacles and dangers in its path.
Hurtling head-on single-mindedly,
Arms flailing, fingers jabbing,
Mouth, tongue and teeth primed and ready.
Wide-eyed, wild eyed,
An admixture of delight, wonder and purpose.
An early life form
Taking its first unassisted steps.

*Robert Deluty*

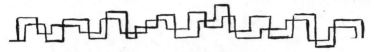

# Duck and Cover

## by Carmella Van Vleet

You have to admit we do some goofy things in the name of parenthood. Have you ever seen a mother trying to get her baby to smile for a photographer in a department store? Standing on her head and singing in front of total strangers. It's embarrassing. The video cameras on the first day of school. Waiting in long lines (or getting in fights) for the latest "hot" toy. And letting Santa bring all the good stuff? What's up with that? But without question the silliest thing I do as a parent is check on my kids before I go to bed.

Each night, ignoring my husband as he shakes his head, I head down the hallway to my children's bedrooms. I creep into my daughter's room and inevitably end up losing the Don't Wake the Baby game. It simply does not matter how softly I sneak or slowly I tread; Abbey stirs. Sometimes, if I freeze, I get lucky and she mumbles quietly and rolls back over with her blankie. More often than not, however, I'm trapped like a soldier behind enemy lines. I have to duck and cover.

Don't tell me you've never done it because I won't believe you. What well-intentioned parent of a baby over six months old *hasn't* dropped to the floor, curled up into a ball right beside a crib, and held her breath when Baby caught him or her coming for a midnight kiss? It happened to me just the other night. With a cheek pressed into the rough carpet and a cramp in my leg all I could think was, "This is ridiculous! I'm a

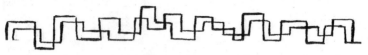

grown woman!" Still, I tried not to move or breathe. I felt like those characters in *Jurassic Park* who insisted that their pal, Tyrannosaurus Rex, wouldn't be able to see them as long as they stayed absolutely, positively motionless. As Abbey stood at the end of her bed, calling softly "Mah-mee, Mah-mee," I knew I had two choices. I could either give myself up and comfort her or wait her out and hope that she'd go back to sleep. Call me crazy or ambitious but I chose the latter.

While I waited for my daughter to lie back down and then for her breath to become slow, even and deep again, I came up with a theory. I'm convinced that the whole "There's a monster under my bed" stage is the direct result of the first cave baby noticing a rock that looked suspiciously like his cave mommy next to his bed of straw. When the poor little thing called out and no one answered, what other conclusion could he draw except that there was some kind of scary blob of a creature that stalked you at night.

Of course, after Abbey settled down I had another problem: how to get out of the room without making too much noise and starting the process all over again. Careful to avoid the creaking floorboards, I made it to the door. Next dilemma: Do I open the door and crawl out on all fours and hope that the hall light doesn't disturb the baby? Or do I try the stand, open and shut swiftly approach? Again I chose the latter. Afterward I waited a moment or two with my hand resting on the doorknob, listening.

Success.

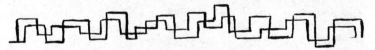

I let the latch click gently into place and headed for my boys' bedroom. When I pulled the blankets up around my middle child, Sammy, he woke up and asked me to sleep with him. I didn't mind. I've gotten untangling myself from my sleeping four-year-old's arms and legs, rolling off the bottom bunk and making it out of the room down to a science. It's his brother's top bunk bed I haven't been able to figure out yet.

# Seasons
## of Life

# Handy (Sandy) Hints

### by Amy Krahn

At long last, summer is here. And so is the sand, the bane of every mother's existence. Outside, it is Mother's little helper—a pile of warm, gritty fun that can keep children occupied for hours on end. The next best thing to a mud puddle. Unfortunately, it doesn't stay outside. Grain by grain, it finds its way inside, clinging to sticky fingers, hiding in pockets, hitching a ride in pant cuffs, insinuating its way into diapered bottoms. Until, eventually, there is more sand in the kitchen than in the whole Mojave Desert.

I have tried everything to stem the flow: stripping my children bare before they come inside, stripping them bare before they go outside, keeping a soft-bristle paint brush at the back door for brushing off stubborn feet and bottoms. I even refused to put sand in the sandbox one year, to no avail—there was plenty of sand in the park.

Well, I am here to say that I have found the solution this year. I give up. I concede defeat. Instead of futilely expending time and energy keeping the sand where I think it belongs, I have decided to harness this previously unrecognized natural wonder product and put it to work for me. Surely there must be some benefit to having all that sand around. I merely need to adjust my outlook, shape up my attitude, change my perspective. Following are a few helpful hints I have discovered to

get you started on your new, happier coexistence with sand.

Sand in the sink? No problem. Add a dollop of liquid soap and you have a powerful abrasive cleaner (abrasive being the key word here.) Works just dandy on the vintage sinks in my house, although I wouldn't recommend it for fiberglass.

Sand in the tub? You're not looking at a dirty tub—you are looking at an exfoliating bath. Who needs a week at a spa? (Okay, we all do. I'll rephrase that—who can afford a week at a spa?) In the privacy of your own home, as you wiggle in the grit on the bottom of the tub, you receive an exfoliating skin treatment that leaves your skin fresh and glowing. (Unfortunately, a fresh and glowing derriere has limited usefulness, but there is potential here. C'mon, think positive—it's free!)

On the kitchen floor? If there's enough of it, and there will be, it helps soak up those nasty juice spills.

In the sheets? I can't help you with this one. Some things simply defy positive thinking.

I think you are beginning to get the picture, though. Like so many of the situations we face day in and day out, we have a choice—we can enjoy life, or we can spend all our time cleaning up after it. We can stomp and scream and brandish our vacuum cleaners, or we can kick back and wiggle our toes in a pile of soft, warm sand—even if it is in the middle of the living room floor.

# Please Don't Make Me Go

### by Laura M. Jones

As my children and I left the coffee hour at my church one Sunday last winter, I spotted a bulletin board with brochures for a nearby church camp.

"Hold on a minute, kids. I want to get one of these," I said, not expecting the gasp of fear that immediately came from my eight-year-old daughter, Rachel.

"NO! NO! You're going to make us go to that!" she sobbed.

"Rachel, it's just a brochure! I just want to look at it. No one is going to make you go. I thought maybe we could drive over for the open house this spring and take a look at the place. Maybe you will want to go some other year when you're older." I was shocked at her reaction; she was the member of the family who was always ready to try new things, who was supremely confident in everything she did.

Rachel was continuing to cry, with occasional pronouncements of "I know you and Dad are going to make us go," when her ever-cautious eleven-year-old brother spoke up.

"I think it sounds like fun," Nate said.

I worked hard to hide my first reaction, which was to shake this alien and demand to know what he had done with my son. "Well," I replied as calmly as I could manage, "I'm sure it is a lot of fun. We can look at the brochure at home, see how much it costs, and consider all the details."

We walked down the corridor and out to the parking lot. I smiled and spoke to friends and acquaintances as Nate tried to divert me from getting into any conversations that would delay our departure. Rachel sobbed quietly and tried to sneak the brochure away from me and into the trash.

We reached the car. "Rachel," I pleaded, "No one is going to make you go to camp!"

Nate, in the front seat next to me, began reading the brochure aloud as I started the short drive home.

"Canoeing, bonfires, cooking over campfires, hikes in the woods, swimming every day, games, songs, five boys and five girls with a male and female counselor in each unit, platform sleeping areas up in the trees. It sounds great. Do you think I can go? If only ten kids can go, don't you think we better sign up today? Please? Can we do it as soon as we get home?"

I explained that there would be more than one unit, so that there would be more space than he thought, and that first I needed to discuss all this with his father.

From the back seat came a quivering voice. "Just how long would we have to go for?" said Rachel, sniffling.

I recognized this as the first crack in the wall. At a stoplight, I looked through the schedule for the coming summer. "Let's see. Nate's age group can go for one

week or two. Probably one week is better for your first time. Rachel, here's one session for your age that is just three days. That wouldn't be too bad, would it?"

There was silence from the back. I waited. Would she dive for cover or forge ahead?

She chose her direction. "I'm not only going for three days if Nate gets to go for a week!"

I looked straight ahead at the road and hid my laughter. "We will have to talk to your Dad about this, and look at the summer schedule, and all that. We'll see if this will all work out."

We pulled into our driveway. The kids jumped out of the car and ran into the house, calling "Dad! Dad! We're going to Camp Glenkirk!"

When the children had gone to change clothes, my husband looked at me with amazement. "How did you talk Nate into this?" he asked.

# Swimmer's Gear

To the pool
We gaily trek
With goggles, towels
And keys 'round my neck.

Two bags are bulging
With toys and fruit,
Kids lead in,
I forgot—
my
suit!

*Gayle Urban*

# The Camp Across the Road

## by Chris Graham

**I** had said this would be our "shake-down" camp out, but I thought I was kidding. Five hours in, we were pretty well shaken down already. It was hot. The four-hour drive had been too long for our youngsters. Although it was still early in the day, we had to settle for the campsite in full sun, next to the banging restroom door. (Maybe we shouldn't have stopped at the locally famous cafe with the scrumptious pies.) Another mom and her family had obviously just beaten us to the last really great spot, and they were unloading across the road from the facilities, under one of two large, shady trees. Their out-of-state license plates showed they had probably been on the road at least four days, and they still looked like a picture out of the L.L. Bean catalog. Oh well.

I slammed together some sandwiches, and my husband and I began tackling the instructions for our new tent. The gnats were amazing. Our kids settled happily into eating chips, pickles, and gnats. I hoped gnats were a good source of protein. As we finally raised the tent poles correctly, I glanced over at the mom across the way. Her kids were happily munching a balanced, gnat-free meal inside the screened porch of their shaded tent. I began taking mental notes. At our camp we chased paper napkins. My husband took a nap in the

sweltering tent. Our one-year-old refused to nap. The sun shone. We sat under a tree, and I mumbled through a stack of picture books in a futile effort to keep the kids controlled and the gnats out of my teeth.

Across the road the other mom did something I've long wished to do. She cloned herself. Another car from the same distant state drove up, and the efficient camp soon was doubled under the second tree. I stood guard, denied cookies, issued drink after drink, looked longingly across the road and began a lengthy mental list for subsequent camp outs: 1. bring balls, 2. bring bubbles, 3. bring *no chips*. The kids across the way happily amused themselves in the shade. OK, several of them were older than mine. Another item for my list: 4. wait five years.

The camp out wore on. The kids would have been happier in our backyard. They moaned through the supposedly nap-inducing air-conditioned scenic drive. One fell asleep as we reached the trail head of the hike and was too groggy to go far. As we cajoled them onward, I imagined the two perfect moms warbling "I love to go a-wandering" with their happy brood.

When we returned to camp, the aroma of dinner across the road blended with the smoke from our tinder. Our dinner was late, half-raw and soaked by a sudden thunderstorm, but the kids revived a little. We dragged them on a walk around the campground. The wildlife was great. We even saw skunks. As night fell, I could see my husband's mental list was getting longer

than mine. I suspected it began: 1. put up ad to sell nearly-new tent.

Across the road, the moms relaxed, chatted, shared stimulating adult conversation after putting the children to bed. We said, "Be quiet!" seven hundred times in increasingly frenzied whispers, and I sang lullabies I didn't even know far into the night.

I awoke to the cheery banging of the restroom door and the smell of bacon, eggs and biscuits wafting my way from the model camp across the road. Blearily I stumbled across the grass with my hand towel and a bottle of dish detergent (list item number 239: bring a bar of bath soap). In the noisy campground restroom I overheard two moms whose voices sounded almost familiar.

"I'd wear a sleeveless blouse," said one, "but they're all lost under the crumbs and junk in our van. I can't find anything."

"These kids," sighed the other. "They say they want a big breakfast, then they run off watching marmots and don't eat a thing."

"I'm sorry," I explained from behind the suds, "but you looked so under control over there. I was taking mental notes on what to do if we ever camp out again."

Recognizing me, they began to laugh. "You're from that cute little camp across the road. The one where the little blond kids were chasing napkins like butterflies. We saw you sitting under the tree reading them stories. We've been taking notes on *you*!"

Suddenly, the morning was delightful. Our family hiked two miles to a spectacular natural arch, proceeding from number to number on the interpretive nature trail. The kids enjoyed it a lot, and are still proud of their accomplishment. We had a grand time watching deer during our picnic lunch and a reasonably peaceful drive back to the city.

As we pulled into the driveway, I thought of those two moms heading across four more days of campgrounds and wished them as many lovely mornings. We were smoky, splotchy and sweaty, but even from our crumb-filled station wagon we looked pretty good.

# Sung Through the Eyes of a Child

### by Kathy E. Smith

This morning, Alex, age four, came to me and asked, "Mom, can you sing the ads for Rudolph?"

"Ads?" I repeated, somewhat stupidly.

"Yeah, Mom, you know the one."

Guessing wildly, I started out, "You know Dasher, and Dancer, and Prancer, and Vixen... "

"Yes, Mom, you got it!" Alex cried excitedly, and continued on with his favorite song about Santa and that most important reindeer flying through the sky on one "froggy Kipsmus eve." To the great delight of his elder siblings, he wound up his performance with, "Then how the reindeer loved him, As they shouted out with me, Rudolph the Red-nosed Reindeer, You'll get down in history!"

As I smiled to myself, I was reminded of a scene from my own childhood. In my early teens, I was a member of a jazz chorus whose leader had tried desperately to impress upon us the importance of enunciation during performances. During one of her lectures, she told us about a child who, when requested to illustrate "Silent Night," drew a picture of the stable, the animals, the angels and a short fat man standing in the corner. When asked to explain, the child replied, "Why, that's round John Virgin!" (The story made perfect

193

sense to me, as I could clearly remember wondering why the Holy Infant slept so well in heavenly peas when the very smell of peas was enough to make me gag.)

The chorus director went on to tell us about the child who sang, "God bless America, Land that I love, Stand beside her, And guide her, Through the night with a light from a bulb." That night when I passed the stories on to my mother, she laughed and said, "You know, when you were quite small, I heard chuckles around us during one church service as the congregation was singing the hymn, 'Bringing in the Sheaves.' With a little child's way of turning the unknown into the familiar, you were bellowing out your own version: 'Jumping in the leaves, Jumping in the leaves, We shall come rejoicing, Jumping in the leaves!'"

I've thought about her comment many times since, particularly when my own children have misspoken familiar lines. Yes, sometimes we do have to worry about whether they're hearing well, correct their mispronunciations so no one teases them, and help them memorize words in the correct order. But sometimes, we need to just lighten up and listen. In their need to translate our adult words into simple concepts they understand, children come up with marvelous interpretations that can cast new meaning on dreary repetition, if only we open our ears to hear it.

Listen, is that Alex singing again? It is! "You'll be ancient, I'll be Carol, Fa la la la la, la la la la."

# The Nutcracker: Men in Tights

### by Francesca Huemer Kelly

*"The children were nestled all snug in their beds,*
*While visions of sugar plums danced in their heads..."*

**I** simply can't help it: Clement Moore's famous poem conjures up my ideal family Christmas. However, my son just handed me his Christmas list and I'm not seeing any sugar plums on it. Plastic droids, CD-ROM war simulation software, cold hard cash—those things are all on the list.

Was there really a time when kids asked for "oranges and sweetmeats" to be tucked in their little shoes? If so, it wasn't in my lifetime. I have to admit I didn't want Santa bringing me any fruit either.

There was one old-fashioned Christmas tradition I did enjoy, though. My mother took me once to see Tchaikovsky's famous ballet, *The Nutcracker*, at Lincoln Center. The sets were magical, the dancers romantic, the music stirring. Manhattan sparkled with tinsel decorations and silver Christmas trees. Salvation Army Santas rang bells on every corner, and you could buy roasted chestnuts and pretzels from the street vendors. The windows at Lord & Taylor enthralled children and adults alike with their mechanized winter scenes of skaters and snowmen.

With a memory like that, it's no wonder that I don't feel that holiday magic when the new movie releases have names like *'Twas the Fright Before Christmas* or *Venison: When Santa Turned Evil*. Nor do I feel all warm and fuzzy about extended hours and syrupy piped-in music at the mall. That's not what Christmas is "supposed to be."

But memory can be a tricky thing. People tend to edit out the bad, remember only the good, forget that people are human and kids will be kids.

Last Christmas, when tickets for a live performance of *The Nutcracker* went on sale in our rather provincial city far from New York, I called my mother right away.

"Mom! *The Nutcracker* is here! Do you remember when we went together?"

She paused for a moment. "Well, I remember taking one of you children to it. Whoever it was never stopped fidgeting."

Hmm. Not I, certainly.

I was not going to let this window of opportunity pass me by while my four children were still school-aged. Who knew when there'd be another *Nutcracker* in town? I bought the tickets.

Now, it wouldn't be enough just to show up with my kids on performance night. Oh, no. They had to be prepped. Coached. Drilled.

Throughout December, Tchaikovsky's lush harmonies were playing constantly as background music in the house and in the car. We brought out the colorful pop-up *Nutcracker* book for incessant perusal. One day

I persuaded the kids to dance some of the parts, using props like a toy nutcracker and swords for the rat soldiers. (With one girl and three boys, sugar plum fairies were in short supply.)

Another day, full of good intentions, I sat them down on the sofa and started the video version starring Mikhail Baryshnikov and Gelsey Kirkland. Within a very short time—before Baryshnikov even made an appearance—the children drifted away and I was left watching it alone. This was not a good sign.

Yet I was not to be deterred. I explained concert etiquette to them: You don't wiggle in your seat, or loudly announce that you need to use the bathroom.

There would be no popcorn. No giant sodas. This was The Ballet, and it was very, very special.

"Yeah, yeah," they said tiredly whenever I repeated the ballet hype. "We know. It's the ballet. It's very, very special and we gotta be good."

"If we are good," said my oldest son, "can we watch 'Star Trek' when we get home?"

Just when the family was on the verge of cultural overload, the big night arrived. Dressed in our holiday best, we drove downtown. Our excitement grew amidst the jostling of the crowd and the smell of wet wool coats as people poured into the hall out of the December snow.

When the curtain rose and the overture began, my youngest son exclaimed, "Hey, I know this music!" Clara flitted about the stage in a white gown, and a slightly scary Herr Drosselmeier put on a puppet show under the giant Christmas tree. Within three minutes, *The Nutcracker* had us in its spell.

I sneaked a peek at my children's enraptured faces and experienced one of those parental moments that are hard to explain: a mixture of pride and nostalgia, a way of experiencing something over again, but even better this time.

My glow was short-lived.

A whole flock of men in tights bounded onto the stage, and I suddenly realized, too late, the one aspect of classical ballet for which I'd forgotten to prepare my children.

"Mom!" yelped the three boys in alarm.

"Uh, Mom?" asked my adolescent daughter. "Are they wearing any pants?"

"Shhh!" I hissed. "They are wearing tights. See how strong their leg muscles are?"

That kept them quiet for about thirty seconds as they watched ten sets of masculine calf and thigh muscles flex and strain. I recalled asking my mother the same question at Lincoln Center.

"The male form is so beautiful," she had answered, "that it's traditional to show it off as much as possible. It makes all those gorgeous leaps and jumps look even more breathtaking."

Interesting explanation, rather sexist. Ah! Now I finally understand why all those society matrons just adore going to the ballet. Patrons of the arts, indeed.

"Look!" said the youngest boy to his brother, forgetting to whisper. "They have really big—"

"Codpieces," I said quickly. "Those are called codpieces." Or were they dance belts? I couldn't remember, but it didn't matter—whatever they're called, they had completely upstaged the sets, the costumes, the music and even all the other parts of the dancers' anatomy.

"What are they for?" asked my older son.

"To protect the men while they're dancing," I said. I resisted the very great temptation to make a nutcracker joke.

The children soon settled down again and concentrated on the ballet. Finally, the curtain came down to enthusiastic applause.

Our excursion had been a resounding success. All four children were chattering on about it afterward and humming the tunes all the way home.

You might even say that visions of sugar plum fairies danced in their heads.

On Christmas morning, we opened the usual presents: miniature spaceships, bright plaid flannel shirts, and crisp greenbacks in holly-decorated envelopes.

Later we watched some of the *Nutcracker* video, the children nestled snugly around me, now experienced ballet-goers. This time we got great close-ups of all the dancers. No one even mentioned the tights.

# Christmas Eve Toast

They wait for Santa under mauve afghans knitted
With a grandmother's practiced purl and stitch.
Doors apart they can still see each other
  across the hall,
    hide from mom,
      take cover,
        pop up and down and laugh in the pillows.

Anticipation fuels tired ham-stuffed bodies.
There is no point in playing bed sentry.
Dad's annual flying sleigh watch calls for
  one last song,
    drink of water,
      nose kiss,
        pop up and down and wait for quiet sounds.

Exhausted Santa always finds the stamina
To rise to the occasion one more year.
Sleeping peaceful children soon wake, wake us
  with a tug
    race for toys,
      tear paper,
        pop up and down and thank us with their joy.

*Terri G. Scullen*

# The Gingerbread House

### by Nelia Odom

Once there was a mother and two children. The children thought it would be fun to make a gingerbread house for Christmas and the mother, who secretly always had wanted to make a gingerbread house and who had a book that described in detail how easy (not to mention fun) making a gingerbread house was, agreed.

But one doesn't just get up in the morning and whip up a gingerbread house, the mother discovered. Making a gingerbread house is not one project, but many. First one must design the house and make pattern pieces out of cardboard for it. Then the gingerbread dough must be mixed and then it must spend some time in the refrigerator before it is firm enough to roll. Then there is the rolling, cutting, and baking of the dough. Next, the baked pieces have to be set aside for a few days so that they have a chance to harden a bit. Then the icing has to be made and then, finally, the house can be built. If it actually stands up it is time to go to the store and buy candy for decorating it.

Fortunately, it was still two weeks before Christmas, so the mother was undaunted, and the children never had been daunted in the first place. The next morning it was wet and cold and grey and snowy—an ideal day to stay inside and bake gingerbread. "Who wants to bake gingerbread today?" asked the mother. "We do!" said the children. So it was agreed.

First they had to design the house and make the pattern pieces. "I want it to have six stories!" said one of the children. "Let's build a deck off the back," said the other child. "Yeah, don't forget the garage! And the balcony!" "How about we be happy with four walls and a roof?" the mother suggested. That sounded fairly pedestrian to the children, but as the supply of cardboard was limited (not to mention the mother's patience) they set to work and soon made a pattern for a basic, respectable gingerbread house.

Next they mixed the dough. They decided to skip the boring step of chilling it in the refrigerator and proceeded to roll it out. They cut out two front and back pieces, two side pieces, and two roof pieces. "Can I eat that big piece when it comes out of the oven Mom?" asked one of the children. "That's the roof," said the mother. "Of course you can't eat it." "Well what can we eat then?" asked the children. "Why don't you roll out the dough scraps and cut them with cookie cutters," suggested the mother. So they did. And then they ran out into the snow to play.

When the mother took the gingerbread house pieces out of the oven she noticed that they had spread a bit on the cookie sheets. "Put pattern pieces over warm gingerbread and trim to fit," advised her book. But by now the mother's gingerbread-making attention span was beginning to wane. "Close enough," she said to herself, and she made a cup of coffee and ate some of the gingerbread cookies the children had made.

A week passed and there was only one week left until Christmas. "Aren't we going to finish the gingerbread house, Mom?" asked the children. "Good idea," said the mother, who had decided that if nobody mentioned it again she could always throw the pieces away after Christmas. "Maybe tomorrow after we get back from our trip. This year we're going downtown to see the Christmas decorations at the White House."

The decorations at the White House were very impressive, especially the large gingerbread house in the State Dining Room, made by the White House pastry chef. It was more of a gingerbread village, actually, complete with elves, trees, and animals, all made of gingerbread. Very, very clever.

Back home, the mother mixed up a batch of royal icing to glue the house pieces together. "Icing should be stiff," cautioned the mother's book. "Plan to work quickly as it dries rapidly." The mother's icing wasn't exactly stiff, but she knew she had measured the ingredients correctly and her attention span was beginning to wane again. "Good enough," she said to herself, and she called her children into the kitchen to help her.

"Can I have a spoonful of that icing?" one of them asked. "No way," the mother replied. She had food phobias about anything made with uncooked egg. "You mean we can't *eat* it?" asked the children, incredulously. "What good is it then?" "It's a decoration," explained the mother. "Can't we even eat the *candy*?" asked the children. "What candy?" said the mother.

"First we have to make this thing stand up. Then we talk about candy."

They iced the edges of the gingerbread house with the icing, and they stood the pieces up next to each other and pressed them together. But they didn't fit! Not exactly, anyway. There were big gaps where the front was supposed to join the side wall, and where the roof pieces joined with each other. "We'll just fill in these cracks with the icing," said the mother. But the icing was runny, not stiff, and it ran down the sides of the house. "Hold these pieces together until the icing dries," said the mother, scraping up the extra icing. "This doesn't look like the one we saw at the White House," observed one of the children, taking his hands off the pieces and standing back to get a better look. Whereupon the house immediately fell apart.

They tried again. Eventually the children went out to play while the mother stood in the kitchen and held onto the house for nearly a half an hour, but finally the icing dried and the house held together. It still didn't look like the one at the White House—it was kind of smeary and battered looking, but at least it was standing up. "Now can we go buy the candy?" asked the children when they came back in. But the mother had had enough of gingerbread houses for the day and Christmas was still nearly a week away. "Later," she said. "There's time."

The naked gingerbread house sat on the sideboard in the dining room until December 23rd when the children asked, "Aren't we going to decorate it, Mom?

When are we going to buy the candy? You *said* . . ."

"Right," the mother interrupted. "Let's go buy the candy."

They put on their coats, went to the grocery store, and came back forty-five minutes later carrying a bag full of a hotly debated assortment of candy. "How do we make it stick on, Mom?" asked the younger child. "With glue, of course," replied the more knowledge-able older child, who was already rummaging through the drawers in search of some. "Not glue, exactly," said the mother. "Remember that icing?"

While the mother made the icing the children opened the bags of candy and began eating. "Save some for the house," the mother cautioned them. She made the icing plenty stiff and when it was ready she gave a dish of it to each child and a knife to spread it with. Then she went into the living room and sat down and looked at the Christmas tree. So much left to do in the next day and a half! Her gingerbread house enthusiasm was more or less gone. Not the children's, though—she could hear them out in the kitchen, engrossed in their project and happily feasting on unrationed candy.

After a while the children called, "Mom, come look!" She went back into the kitchen and there stood a fin-ished gingerbread house! "Isn't it beautiful?" exclaimed the older child, who was actually jumping up and down with pleasure. "I like it *better* than the one at the White House." "Let's never eat it," said the younger child. "Let's save it for every Christmas. Do you think we can keep it *forever*, Mom?"

The mother looked around the kitchen, at the icing hardening all over the counter, at the crushed candy on the floor, at the pleased, excited children, at the newly colorful gingerbread house, miraculously still standing beneath an incredible load of candy. She stood there and took it all in and promised herself that she'd always remember this scene. "Yes," she said with assurance. "I'm sure I will keep this forever."

Coming to Terms

# Why I Never Wrote
### by Marybeth McPherson

**I** became a *Welcome Home* subscriber over four years ago. After reading my first issue from cover to cover I thought, *I was an English major. I can write. I'll send in an article about life with a toddler son.* I jotted down some ideas in a notebook. Before I found time to write the article, I found out I was pregnant. Exhaustion took hold. I wanted to write, but I *really* wanted to sleep. My toddler son covered the pages of that notebook with crayon art. So ended my first attempt to write for *Welcome Home.*

Then my second son was born. After the first hectic months with a two-year-old and an infant, life settled down somewhat and I thought again of writing. This time the topic would be "Fashion for At-Home Mothers of Infants and Preschoolers"—something about how spit-up was being worn on the right shoulder this year and which colors provide the best camouflage when you're being used as a human tissue during cold and flu season. I started a rough draft in a hard cover journal one night. Shortly after that my father-in-law, who lived with us, underwent hip surgery. This caused a general upheaval in our home, with health aides and physical therapists coming and going. I didn't see that journal again until a year later, when we were packing up our household to move.

Moving with a four-year-old and an almost two-year-old—now that would have been a good subject. I

could have shared helpful hints. But who had time to write? Who could even find a pen? When unpacking and settling in with preschoolers the priorities are toys, dishes, and more toys. (That's a helpful hint.) I listed a few notes on a piece of packing paper, but it must have been taken out for recycling.

One year later, on Mother's Day, *The Boston Globe* ran a feature claiming daughters whose mothers work outside the home have higher self-esteem and more respect for their moms than do daughters of at-home mothers. I responded with a letter to the editor about my high self-esteem and my excellent relationship with my own mother, who had stayed home to raise her children. *The Globe* published my letter and several of my friends commented on it. Emboldened by that experience, I was again ready to write for *Welcome Home*, perhaps expanding on the subject of my letter. But instead of working on an article in tribute to my mother, I threw her a big seventieth birthday party. I know she would have been flattered and touched by the article, but she had a great time at the party.

We got a computer that Christmas. Now I had the tools I needed to compose a really good piece of writing. I wanted to write about my youngest son's obsession with Clifford the Big Red Dog. He actually thought he was Clifford. I was getting pretty tired of making bone sandwiches and pretending that I was Emily Elizabeth, his owner. I was typing along nicely one afternoon, but when I stepped away to help my older son in the bathroom, Clifford pressed a few keys and wiped the whole thing out. Bad dog!

Soon after that attempt at publication, I became pregnant again. My sister was three months ahead of me, expecting twins. We were excited about being pregnant at the same time, and I eagerly anticipated writing about our experiences. Unfortunately, I miscarried. I lost interest in composing and instead concentrated on healing and on appreciating my two beautiful sons.

My sister later gave birth to two healthy sons of her own. I planned to draft some guidelines on life with two boys, something she could refer to as her sons grew. I could even expand it into an article. Instead, I baked her six dozen cookies, a loaf of strawberry bread and a turkey pie. She needed the energy more than the education.

Which brings me to today. I just read the latest issue of *Welcome Home* cover-to-cover and that old feeling came over me again. *Oh, no,* I cautioned myself, *don't even think about it.* After all, there are a million reasons why I will never complete an article for submission. If you don't believe it, I'll list them.

Wait a minute....

# New Wardrobe

My suit
Thai silk, royal blue,
custom-made on a business trip to Bangkok
droops from the hanger,
the cleaner's bag peeled off,
removed from the small children
who crouch among the dusty shoes
during their game of hide and seek.

When they were born,
my daughters shucked my body
like an old sock,
leaving me baggy and wrinkled,
unfit for gathered waists
or anything tailored.

I bulked up on sweatpants and tees,
the perfect blotter
for sticky fingers and spit-up,
shoved my best suits
to the back of the closet,
surrendered the workday outfits
for dress-up.

Now they pretend to be ladies
in challis skirts, wool slacks, silk jackets,
preening and giggling in the mirror,
my days of vanity in wrinkles
trampled by small feet
in high heels.

*Clara Silverstein*

# The Strong-Willed Parent

### by Susan Bolton Burger

**E**arly one recent morning, I was embroiled in the usual breakfast skirmish with my two young children when, all of a sudden, the Be-Careful-What-You-Wish-For Fairy caught me in a moment of weakness. An unexpected phone call came offering my younger child a place at our local preschool. Now, for two brief mornings a week, I bask in sheer, unadulterated adulthood for the first time in two-and-a-half years.

Well, mostly I just drink *entire* cups of tea and glue the furniture back together, but I have plans to bask. Until then, I rest bold and briefly in the eye of the storm.

For the last two years, my younger child and I have gone toe-to-toe around the clock. According to lofty books on parenting perplexities, he's a "strong-willed child." With that firm grasp of the obvious to bolster me, I read on to discover that there is no known cure. Scientists aren't even working on it.

God kissed this child, laughed heartily and sent him down to me, a mother with her own peevish disposition. I must accept this.

Please understand. For several years, I sat smugly secure in the knowledge that I had motherhood licked. Clearly, I was born to nurture.

My daughter, sweet-tempered and biddable from birth, is the envy of friends with less agreeable children. She can sit quietly in a restaurant, even in front of in-laws, has never assaulted another child and will probably do our taxes and clean the gutters without asking before she hits the second grade. But that summer evening two years ago, while I was straining to pat myself on the back, I was rudely interrupted by a formidable night nurse. She graciously served me a big fat slice of humble pie in Pampers® and said, with a twinkle, "He's a corker!"

From that day to this, it has been hand-to-hand combat with a testosterone-charged miniature of myself. "He's *your* son," I bellow at my affable spouse, while we retrieve, repair or reprimand our Y chromosome. But nobody's fooled. Every time his lower lip goes out and his chubby heels dig in, I face my own face. Our once disciplined home now sounds like a *Wild Kingdom* out-take. Play dates, once plentiful, are now scarce—delightful refreshments sit neglected in favor of a referee with first aid skills, and only the truly loyal ever return to our address. As for the babysitter, we pay her copious sums and drive away quickly, but you can bribe your mother just so often.

So with fear on my face, hope in my heart, and two pounds of ground Cheerios® under my floor mats, I drove off to preschool last month, ready to launch this child into polite society. But would polite society show us the door and refund our deposit? I prepared for tantrums and tears. Meanwhile, my temperamental tyke

hopped gaily out of the car, beaming like a choirboy at his new teacher. He didn't even glance back as he trotted off with this new authority figure. But there were tears.

Mine, of course—all the way home. I had turned in my stiff upper lip with my slim cut jeans when my first child was born, so tears are no novelty. If you've never tried bawling in your car, you might give it passing consideration. Fellow motorists will frequently let you merge without much discussion.

I cried for the child who has challenged me, changed me and brought several emergency room physicians to their knees. I cried because, for the next three hours, someone else would serve and protect my little storm cloud. But mostly, I cried from the shock of suddenly having *nothing pressing to do*! So I decided to dry up and be grateful—not a natural state for my prickly persona. I am grateful for the painful, priceless lessons of tolerance and empathy that my willful son is teaching me. The hand I used to pat my own back not so long ago is now offered quickly and sincerely to frazzled fellow travelers.

My comprehensive comeuppance inspires me to uncharacteristic political action. Indeed, I have my own ideas for the national budget. Instead of paying taxes for one year, every American household should be tasked with the care and feeding of a strong-willed two-year-old. Those who can thoroughly document prior experience with the above will be cheerfully excused and assigned front row seats to laugh at the

uninitiated. My fellow Americans, I offer assurance that we will emerge a tired, broken, yet pithy citizenry, ready to lead the world in compassion and regular nap schedules. Regrettably, our streets will be littered with the pompous, the self-satisfied and the terminally tidy withering by the wayside, mumbling incoherently about boarding schools and sleep deprivation. We'll need plenty of makeshift detox shelters where these deflated souls can have a long rest and plenty of adult conversation.

Sadly, I can't squeeze in a road trip to Capitol Hill during my three-hour preschool furlough. Unless funds can be raised to airlift me out of the laundry room, my political agenda will have to wait. Sigh. It's time to collect the corker.

# Am I Overqualified or Underqualified for This Job?

**by Rosemary Raymond Horvath**

**F**or a person who majored in piano, I sure do a lot of nursing. For a chef who determines when dinner is ready by whether the smoke alarm went off or not, I am amazed that I prepare over a thousand meals a year. For a woman who is an ardent conservationist, I have a lot of children. And for someone who occasionally adds instead of subtracts in the checkbook, I sure do a lot of money management!

All of these make me feel like a blithering idiot, a jack-of-all-trades, the world's most overburdened unemployed person, or occasionally, absolutely brilliant. I spend hundreds of dollars a month at the grocery store, but I cut each soap pad in half, to make it last longer. What a contradiction!

For years, I have been sewing my children's clothes. I do beautiful work, and it is a source of pride to see my entire family decked out in clothing I made. What possessed me, then, to glue-gun scout badges on? (Trust me. Not a good idea.)

I have taught piano lessons for fourteen years, with four recitals a year, and a waiting list coming out the proverbial kazoo, if not the keyboard. Why then, do all my children want martial arts lessons instead? They

are not mutually exclusive, unless you want time to do something like, say, breathe.

I am a sucker for animals; I'm the neighbor who takes in your ailing hamsters, adopts them, and nurtures them for years, when their lifespan is usually measured in months. We have at any given time a remarkable menagerie, and are the family the school dumps the animals on for the summer. We never take vacations because we are babysitting other people's pets. This is a little odd, because I am horribly allergic to most animals, and spend hours every day tending my nose.

I have never considered myself particularly patient; I get annoyed at rude salesclerks, don't tolerate sassiness in children, and long for a shiny kitchen floor. Why, then, is it my house that comes unglued at 3:30 each afternoon, when my children and everyone else's too come home to spread popcorn all over my house? I am bored to tears by card games (I lose track halfway through and forget whether it's bridge or poker; the cards all look the same to me) so why am I always on the floor with some kid (often not even my own) putting together puzzles or gluing legs back on a spider?

Anyone who has ever known me will tell you that I am a patron of the arts, and though I am healthy, I am not an athlete. I worked for two years for the coaches at the University of Arizona in college days, and never went to a game. Tell me, does it seem bizarre that I am coaching a soccer team these days?

I have always taken pride in my appearance; I wear makeup each day, and curl my hair. How did it happen, then, that I once went to church, sang in the choir, and came home before I realized that I had forgotten to take my "Kiss the Cook" apron off? I thought everyone was smiling at me because it was a beautiful day! I also went to school one day wearing a Viking helmet I'd forgotten to take off. But at least the children mentioned this one to me (with great hilarity).

I guess having children is such an overwhelming experience, so all-consuming and so marvelous, that the person you used to be isn't adequate. You grow with each child and you learn parallel lessons with each child. Obviously, with five children, my learning curve is really steep!

So I continue to worry about pennies and fritter away the dollars on things like braces and flowers (equally important to me), I darn socks on my sewing machine, then hand smock a dress, and I continue to call in the children for dinner with my handy smoke alarm. And some days I'm competent, and some days I'm not!

# About
# Family and Home Network™

Founded in 1984 as Mothers At Home, **Family and Home Network** is a national nonprofit 501C(3) organization whose mission is to:

★ Advocate for parents and children of all ages concerning their need for generous amounts of time together;

★ Affirm the choice to be home through the many stages of parenthood to nurture children of all ages;

★ Provide parent-to-parent support, education and networking;

★ Correct society's misconceptions and refute stereotypes about parenting;

★ Encourage respect for the contributions made by each parent, as couples share decisions regarding nurturing and providing for their families;

★ Empower all parents to preserve and improve the opportunity to forgo or cut back on paid employment; and

★ Educate society about the benefits of parents and children being emotionally engaged and spending generous amounts of time together.

We have profound respect for parents who make the commitment to spend generous amounts of time with their children. We advocate for universal recognition of the critical importance of this work and acknowledgement of the short- and long-term benefits to society.

**Other Publications**

*Welcome Home®*, our award-winning journal, brings affirmation and information each month in its beautifully illustrated, advertisement-free pages. *Welcome Home* includes personal essays expressing the joys and challenges of parenthood, informative articles about family life and health, parent-to-parent problem solving, media watch and public policy articles, original artwork and photographs, humorous stories, poetry and more. Written, edited and illustrated by parents, *Welcome Home* invites parents everywhere to join its thoughtful and caring community.

Deep feelings and powerful insights are eloquently expressed in our book *Motherhood: Journey Into Love*. Our poetry editor selected more than seventy of the best-loved poems from the pages of *Welcome Home* to trace the journey of motherhood from conception through grandparenting. Over thirty talented artists contributed their work to enhance this moving and meaningful collection.

*Discovering Motherhood* was created by the staff of Family and Home Network especially for women in their first years of motherhood. The editors realized that new mothers, faced with significant physical, emotional and social changes, are especially in need of assistance while they make the transition into motherhood. *Discovering Motherhood* explores the realities and rewards of a home-centered life. Lovely drawings illustrate the personal narratives, essays, informative articles, humor and poetry from more than forty authors.

"Best of" collections from *Welcome Home* are designed to provide information when you need it. Covering the topics most often requested by *Welcome Home* readers, the collections include essays, resource information and parent-to-parent problem solving. They range in length from one to six articles, and are priced accordingly. Request a list of our "Best of" collections by mail, or see our website for descriptions of each collection: www.FamilyAndHome.org.

### Speaking Out for Parents

In addition to publishing *Welcome Home* and our books, an important part of our work is educating the public, members of the media and policymakers about families who care for their own children and about the needs of children of all ages. Our staff and volunteers have spoken at Congressional hearings and at policy conferences, as well as in thousands of media interviews. Issues that impact our families are complex—tax policies, child care subsidies, social security reforms—and we work to ensure that policy makers and the media understand the range of choices families make in caring for their children. Powerful lobbying organizations (funded by corporations, charitable foundations and education and labor groups) look out for the interests of parents who are employed full-time and using childcare. We are here to speak up for families who provide all or most of the care for their own children, for those who want to provide care for their own children, and most important, for all children, who need generous amounts of nurturing time with their parents.

## A Family-Friendly Organization

The Family and Home Network volunteers and staff have work options which include part-time and job-share positions, flexible schedules, flex-time and home-based work. The organization is housed in a family-friendly office that includes a large playroom and a high tolerance for noise, crayons, spills and frequent interactions with children.

## Contact Family and Home Network

You may contact us at:

Family and Home Network
9493-C Silver King Court
Fairfax, Virginia 22031
(703) 352-1072
e-mail: admin@FamilyAndHome.org

Please visit our website at **www.FamilyAndHome.org**

Or call our information line: **(866) 352-1075**
for a free info packet.